TEACHING AND LEARNING AS A
COMMUNICATION PROCESS

TEACHING AND LEARNING AS A COMMUNICATION PROCESS

PHILIP HILLS

CROOM HELM LONDON

© 1979 P.J. Hills
Croom Helm Ltd, 2-10 St John's Road, London SW11

British Library Cataloguing in Publication Data

Hills, Philip James
    Teaching and learning as a communication process.
    1. Communication in education   2. Teaching
    I. Title
    371.1'02   LB1027

    ISBN 0-85664-701-2

Printed in Great Britain by offset lithography by
Billing & Sons Ltd, Guildford, London and Worcester

CONTENTS

TO FRANCES

THE PURPOSE OF THIS BOOK

This book is intended to be of use to all those engaged in teaching and learning in higher, further and continuing education. It considers teaching and learning as a communication process, distilling out some practical guidelines for closer communication between the teacher and the student.

Chapter 1 sets the scene by looking at the growth of the formal education system while Chapter 2 considers a model of teaching and learning as a communication process which consists of three main parts: teacher processes, channels of communication, and student processes.

Chapter 3 regards this from the psychological aspect and Chapters 4, 5 and 6 look at verbal and non-verbal communication, audio-visual communication and interpersonal and group communication respectively. Chapter 7 considers varieties of mass communication both historically and from the point of view of future trends which might affect teaching and learning.

Chapters 8 and 9 are concerned with the student as receiver of the communication and the teacher as sender of the communication. This is seen in terms of the inputs of information to the student, the outputs that he or she must make and the internal processes that need to be considered.

Chapter 10 looks again at the three parts of the communication process in terms of specific guidelines for the preparation of effective teaching/learning materials.

For ease of reference to specific areas the book ends with a summary of the main points. For those who wish to explore these areas in more detail, selected references have been given in the section on 'further reading'.

My thanks are due to: the McGraw-Hill Book Company for permission to quote a passage from J.A. Peddiwell, *The Saber-tooth Curriculum*, New York, 1939; *Theory into Practice* for permission to quote from Volume X, No. 4, October 1971; A.M. Love and J.A. Roderick, *Teacher Nonverbal Communication: The Development and Field Testing of an Awareness Unit*, p. 296; J. Victoria, *A Language for Affective Education*, p. 302; Pan Books Ltd for permission to quote from my book *Study to Succeed*, 1973, p. 61; Tetradon Publications

Ltd for permission to quote from L. Haynes, P. Groves, R. Moyes
and P. Hills, 1977, *Effective Learning: A Practical Guide for Students,*
Tetradon Publications, Bridge House, Shalford, Guildford, Section 8.4.

I should like to thank all those teachers and students who have
commented on or who have been exposed to the various parts of the
text. Thanks also to my wife and son who have helped in so many
ways.

P.J. Hills
Guildford, 1978

1 HUMAN COMMUNICATION AND THE EDUCATION PROCESS

In the last chapter of my book, *The Self-Teaching Process in Higher Education*, I quote the final report of the Carnegie Commission on Higher Education, published in 1973, which sets out what it considers to be the main purposes of higher education. These include:

> enhancing human capacity in society at large through training, research, and service . . .

> advancing learning for its own sake through science, scholarship and creative arts; and for the sake of public interest and consumption . . .

> evaluating society, for the benefit of its self-renewal, through individual scholarship and persuasion.

All of these purposes imply a communication between society and the individual. Indeed, so it is with all formal education. In essence, society is concerned through its education system with acquiring knowledge and skills, transmitting its values and standards to the coming generation to safeguard the existence of that society.

The purpose of education in ancient Greece was exactly this, to safeguard society by education in two main areas: the attainment of physical fitness and the preservation of religious and moral standards. Well into the fifth century BC the educational ideal of Athens was the soldier-citizen. It is interesting to note that after the Persian wars Athens became not just a warrior state, but a thriving industrial and commercial business centre. This had a great effect on its ideas of education. There grew an educational system which combined areas of religion, intellect, artistry and aestheticism.

This pattern of communication through education is repeated again and again in different contexts throughout the ages as the needs and standards of society change, and is continuing even more so today all over the world. Indeed, the technology of modern communications is being made use of in formal education for the same purposes as evidenced by the instructional television satellite experiment in India. The purposes of this experiment were given as 'to emphasise the need for population control, communicate about health, nutrition and the new agricultural methods and to create scientific awareness amongst the people' (Chaudri, 1977). The use of the satellite enables a range of villages located in different regions of the country to be reached.

Education can thus be seen as a communication process between society and the individual, but we need to keep this in mind when looking at our formal system of education, as there is a constant need to consider relevance. Education must be looked at constantly to determine how well it is communicating the standards of society and the store of man's knowledge.

It is not the intention of this book to consider what these standards are, nor what amongst the store of man's knowledge is worthy and necessary for transmission to maintain that society. Instead the chapters which follow will concentrate on the process of communication, looking to see how teachers and students act and interact. First, however, let us look briefly at the past to see the origins of some of these ideas.

To return to what we have learned of some of the earliest ideals in educational thought, i.e. education in ancient Greece, we find that the methods advocated by Socrates in the middle of the third century BC provide one illustration of this idea of interaction which we have just discussed. The Socratic method of instruction was carried out in the form of a guided set of questions and answers through which the teacher sought to lead the student to knowledge and conclusions.

Socrates' intention was to stimulate thought in his 'pupils'. He often pretended ignorance of a point and let his pupil 'teach' him. The whole idea had stemmed from the Greek desire for fluency of speech; out of this need rose the Sophists who travelled the country lecturing on rhetoric. Socrates, influenced by their teaching, took up the challenge and became consequently the most famous teacher in Greece through his dialogue, that is, through communication. His aim was to guide students through various processes of thought to an awareness of truth discovered by themselves. This he did by question and answer and by examples which he gave to his pupils; in fact he taught by an induction method.

Time and time again throughout history, as theories and practice of education developed, we see emphasis on 'self' and the fact that our own senses are there to be used. Comenius in the seventeenth century believed in the extreme necessity of having a 'right way of teaching', in order to give a good grounding in knowledge upon which 'self' development might build. He, like Socrates before him, saw the teacher as the 'centre'. He conceived the idea of a universal education. Education as he saw it was the most complete preparation for life possible. It could only be effective if account was taken of the learner, and therefore instruction had to be fitted to the learner, not the other way round. One could say that in him was the beginning of modern education.

Rousseau in the eighteenth century continued the trend towards the modern idea of education as did others in his era. He too advocated the need for national education; without it there would be no means of making good citizens. It could not be imposed upon them, he believed; the original nature of each child had to be developed. To achieve this Rousseau believed education must be 'solitary', 'rationalist', and 'utilitarian'. His scheme for education was derived from his principle of age-grouping. His main writing on education came in his *Emile*, the story of a boy growing up, and this had an immediate effect in the eighteenth century. People began to adopt his ideas and, what was most important, to realise how fundamental education was to the building of society. They became aware of the necessity of considering new schemes which might improve the educational process.

One might think that the great influence of Rousseau's theories would have smothered the idea of individual development, concerned as he was with the idea of making good citizens. This however is not true as we see when we consider people such as Pestalozzi who, like Rousseau, believed that for the best education good parents and a good home were essential, and that the family was the best example a school could follow. Unlike Rousseau, Pestalozzi saw that the status of the home was not so important. It was the example set by it which mattered, i.e. the example of the parents. When in educational establishments teachers were set in the position of parents at home, that is, as the centre piece and example, the development of the individual was possible. The teacher was the instrument by which ideals and ideas were communicated. From this position he was led to a whole scheme of education.

Each step in the education of an individual must be within the reach of his intellect. The chief weakness in Pestalozzi's system was that he failed to recognise that method had to change for a pupil as he developed. He never considered methods which might be best for those who had mastered the basic elements. This was left to those who followed in an age when the world began a change which is still continuing. Many people, however, consider Pestalozzi to be the founder of the elementary system of education.

The idea of producing 'good men' was the fundamental principle behind education according to Herbart (1776-1834) who too stated a belief in Pestalozzi's methods, though he carried them further. His basic concept was that through knowledge comes morality and towards this end his ideas were directed.

Interest, according to him, was an important factor in the learning process; the student's mind must become absorbed in whatever he was learning. To be boring or bored hindered the whole process of communication from teacher to student: 'interest means self-activity'. Here we have reference to the self-teaching process which is of such interest in the second half of the twentieth century. Herbart is worthy of note here for his idea of four stages in instruction, that is, in the communication process: clearness, association, system, and method. Today these four stages have been developed into five by his advocates: preparation, presentation, association, condensation, and application, and it is necessary for the lecturer and student in the teaching/learning situation to grasp these stages.

The first half of the nineteenth century saw many idealist educators who believed that good communication was essential in the education process. Froebel, though he was to be remembered for his ideas on the education of the very young, had a fundamental concept which can be applied to the whole range of educational progress, that of systematic activity.

The experiments to discover the best system of universal education, so prevalent in the nineteenth century, continued into the twentieth century, and many educators, such as Maria Montessori, established experimental schools. All stress the idea of individual development, that the individual is the important element in the teaching/learning process.

I have merely touched on a few of the outstanding educators of the past, those particularly concerned with enhancing the individual through learning, with advancing learning both for its own sake and for that of the world, endeavouring to create a better man through self-directed education and through complete communication. All through the ages these thinkers have stressed the importance of communication. We shall find traces of these fundamental concepts in the chapters which follow.

2 TEACHING AND LEARNING AS A COMMUNICATION PROCESS

Since the main purpose of this book is to explore teaching and learning and to consider it in terms of a communication process, we shall use this chapter to explore a model which will serve as a framework for later chapters. First, however, let us consider communication itself. Communication can be concerned with the transmission of information between people, animals or machines, or it can be used in the sense that railways and roads are communication networks which enable people to move from place to place. Here we are concerned with the former, the transmission of information between a sender and a receiver.

Let us begin with a communication model intended for application to the development of systems like the telephone, the telegraph, television etc. It was first proposed during the 1940s when the mathematician Shannon became interested in the problem of transmitting accurate messages over a communication channel. The need was to design a system where the difference between signals sent and signals received was low. A model of a communication system was proposed consisting of the following parts:

Input → Coding → Channel → Decoding → Output
                    ↑
               Noise

Shannon subsequently developed this into a more general treatment in collaboration with Weaver, published in their book, *The Mathematical Theory of Communication* (Shannon and Weaver, 1949).

Although this communication model was applied to the development of electrical systems, it can and has been applied to an analysis of human communication. Much work has been done in this area and many books published, such as Parry (1970) and Cherry (1966).

There are two main types of person concerned with communication in teaching and learning: *the teacher as sender of the message* and *the student as receiver of the message.* Thus we may modify the model to show the areas of direct concern for the sender and receiver:

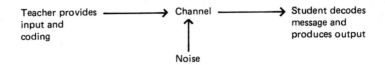

An aspect this modified model omits is 'feedback'. This is an important component of the type of electronic system for which this model was originally intended and it is particularly important in the context of teaching and learning, as will emerge later. However, let us for the moment omit it and consider each of the areas above in a little more detail.

Teacher Provides Input and Coding

Input

We have seen in Chapter 1 how education is the process by which we communicate our knowledge, our standards, our heritage and culture from generation to generation. This is our input, but we must consider a cautionary tale which is well told by Peddiwell in his book *The Saber-tooth Curriculum*' (Peddiwell, 1939).

This story tells of a prehistoric tribe which decided to introduce education to its children in the form of teaching skills designed to meet particular survival needs. The first subject in the curriculum was 'fish-grabbing-with-the-bare-hands', ensuring more and better food by catching fish from the streams and pools of clear water near where the tribe lived. The second subject was 'woolly-horse-clubbing'. The woolly horses came down to the water to drink and grazed in a nearby meadow. Their coats provided skins to keep the tribe warm. The third subject was 'saber-tooth-tiger-scaring-with-fire' using firebrands to keep the tigers away from the water and give the tribe greater security.

In the course of time a new ice age came to that part of the world and a glacier came down from a nearby mountain range. When it came close to the stream that ran through the tribe's valley it began to melt into the stream. The dirt and gravel that the glacier had collected on its long journey dropped into the water, so that it became muddy. Since all the slow-moving fish had been caught by the tribe with their bare hands, only quick-moving fish were left and these were easily able to hide under boulders thrown into the stream by the glacier and dart swiftly and unseen through the muddy water. So no matter how good a man's fish-grabbing education had been he could not grab fish if there were no fish to grab.

The other subjects in the curriculum, horse-clubbing and tiger-scaring, became equally irrelevant as the nature of the land near the glacier changed. The woolly horses died out and the tigers went away, but their place was taken by agile antelopes and ferocious bears. Skills of fish-net-making, antelope-snare construction and bear-catching were developed. But meanwhile, as you have probably guessed, what was still being taught back in the schools was fish-grabbing, woolly-horse-clubbing and tiger-scaring. The teachers in the prehistoric schools were no longer in touch with the needs of their tribe.

The cautionary tale is, of course, that in the fast changing world of today, relevance is of greater importance than it has ever been. There is a great need to ensure that the content and type of our courses in schools and in institutions of higher, further and continuing education are subject to regular review. Much work is being done and has been carried out over the last few years both to consider the relevance of the curriculum in our educational institutions and to take steps to institute curriculum reform. In Great Britain, the Nuffield Foundation Science projects in schools have been one example. The Schools Council has also been considerably active in this area. In addition, the Department of Education and Science has recently set up an Assessment of Performance Unit to monitor mathematics and later language performance in schools.

It is not the purpose of this book to explore the detailed subject inputs to the process and for anyone wishing to read more in the area of curriculum processes the books edited by Harris, Lawn and Prescott (1975) and Golby, Greenwald and West (1975) would act as a starting-point.

Coding

Given that the subject matter input to the process is determined, one can then examine ways in which this is communicated to the student. Regardless of whether teachers generate their own material or whether it is generated by someone else and then used by teachers, the material starts off as an idea inside someone's head which has to be made visible to the student.

In teaching, ideas, statements etc., are displayed either in writing, pictorially (visual communication), or by the spoken word (verbal communication). These are reinforced or modified by a variety of non-verbal messages. Visual, verbal, and non-verbal communication will be considered in later chapters.

Coding is the process of making the desired input visible to the student, and the teacher needs to be concerned that the coding is such that the student is able to receive the material and will be able to understand and decode it.

The teacher makes his ideas visible by coding them into the series of symbols which go to make up spoken or written language or into common pictorial symbols. The essential condition is that the student should speak and understand the same series of symbols. This includes the specialised symbols associated with particular subjects. Does the student understand the meaning of any special words used in the subject? Is the student's background knowledge sufficient for the level at which the teacher is coding the subject? Without the compatability of coding and decoding processes there will be no communication, since symbols can only be representations of events and not the event itself.

Channel

The channel of communication should convey the message to the student accurately. If the teacher is directly concerned with this, he may be using his voice as the channel of communication in conjunction with a variety of visual methods, the simplest of which is perhaps the blackboard. I still remember one of my mathematics lecturers who used to talk at the blackboard while he wrote his notes upon it. As he wrote the notes with one hand he shielded them from view with his body and rubbed them out with the other hand. His channels of communication hardly ever reached the students.

There are now available many varieties of audio-visual equipment which can either be used to aid the teacher or be used for instruction without the teacher in group or individual work by students. On the visual side these range from simple aids like the overhead projector and 35mm slide projector, to ciné projectors, cassette videotape players and computer graphics terminals. On the audio side the most versatile piece of equipment is the audio cassette tape player which can be used in conjunction with much of the visual display equipment. Often, it is found most useful when used in conjunction with simple printed materials. When considering channels of communication apart from the voice, one must not neglect the printed page because this has so many possibilities for presenting textual and diagrammatic materials, both as teacher support material and when designed for individual use as worksheets, programmed material or use with audio-taped material.

The main consideration in choosing the channel of communication is that it should clearly and accurately convey the message to the student. The point previously mentioned should be stressed again here, i.e. that symbols are only representations of events and not the events themselves. Therefore, the message conveyed by the chosen channel of communication can in no way convey the same message the actual event itself could convey. The message conveyed, in addition to being compounded of the choice of symbols selected by the teacher and the way in which they are received by the student, has certain inherent characteristics which are present as a necessary part of the channel of communication chosen. This should perhaps be easiest to see and appreciate if the same subject were to be viewed by projection of a high-definition 35mm colour slide and a relatively low-definition, small screen, black and white television picture. These points will be taken up again in Chapter 5.

Noise

In the original communication model, noise in the system was the sort of thing which renders a telephone conversation unclear or produces crackles on the line masking the speech. The necessity for clarity and accuracy of the message has already been stressed, but in teaching and learning there are many sources of noise that can mask or obscure the message whatever channel of communication is being used.

One quite considerable source of noise is perhaps the teaching environment itself. Too little attention has been paid to date to the large variety of factors which go to make up the teaching environment. Often, the main requirement seems to be that it is a room containing sufficient numbers of chairs and that it has a blackboard or facility for an overhead projector. Qualities of comfort of the chairs, visual impact of the colour of the walls and floor covering, sound quality and spacial dimensions of the room seem to be ignored. All these and more are important if one is considering potential noise in the system.

The size of a group also influences directly the physical noise, since the larger the group the more likely they are to produce noises like sneezes and coughs, chair moving etc. Someone sitting at the back of such a group could have a considerable degree of interference with his reception of the message.

Perhaps the biggest potential source of noise is the teacher himself. Because he is concerned with getting the communication across to his students he must be clear as to his purpose and make sure that the material he prepares is as clear and unambiguous as possible. He must choose appropriate channels of communication, using a variety of techniques to ensure that the students receive and learn the material presented. All these are potential sources of noise in the system.

Student Decodes Message and Produces Output

Teachers expect students coming from school to an institution of higher education to have a sufficient background in a subject to be able to decode the material presented. Students are also often expected to possess skills of notetaking writing up practical work, an ability to use books and extract information from them, and skills of argument and discussion. This is so often obviously not the case.

First, the possession of a recognised qualification in a subject at school level is no guarantee that sufficient background to a subject is possessed. This is not intended to be a criticism of work in schools, it is more a basic criticism of the examination system which inevitably must select certain areas of a syllabus to test, but equally must exclude others. Part of a teacher's task when a student enters a course of instruction should be to determine whether the student does possess sufficient background knowledge and, if he does not, to help him to acquire it.

As to the skills of notetaking, writing up etc., these also cannot be assumed, and teachers would do well to discuss these points with their students, providing help where necessary. These points are taken up in Chapter 8 'The Student as Receiver'.

Feedback

I have already indicated that the concept of 'feedback' had been omitted from the model, but that it was an important part of it. Feedback is an important part of any self-regulating mechanism and, since human beings are largely self-regulating mechanisms, this must be considered in the context of teaching and learning. For the moment our model can be made even simpler:

Message channel

Teacher   Student

Feedback channel

Instead of the process consisting simply of the teacher passing messages to the student, the communication process should be a dynamic interchange with the student feeding back information on how the teacher's messages have been received; as a result of this he can amplify or extend the communication as necessary. The message channel and feedback channel therefore should form a continuous

feedback loop between teacher and student so that the student keeps
the teacher aware of his difficulties and the teacher keeps the student
aware of the student's progress and attempts to solve any difficulties
he may have.

Since the feedback channel is subject to the same sort of factors
as the original model used, the total model we have developed could
be viewed in terms of three main categories:

>   channels of communication
>   student processes
>   teacher processes

Although in the following account there is an inevitable overlap
between the three categories, chapters dealing with these are roughly
as follows:

Channels of Communication

Chapter 3 Psychological Aspects of Communication
Chapter 4 Verbal and Non-Verbal Communication
Chapter 5 Audio-Visual Communication
Chapter 6 Interpersonal and Group Communication
Chapter 7 Varieties of Mass Communication

Student Processes

Chapter 8 The Student as Receiver

Teacher Processes

Chapter 9 The Teacher as Sender

Chapter 10 will examine the conclusions of the above chapters in terms
of these three categories, and for quick reference a summary of the
main points of each chapter has been placed at the end. The bibliography contains details of books to enable anyone who wishes to read
further into particular subjects to do so.

3 PSYCHOLOGICAL ASPECTS OF COMMUNICATION

In the teaching and learning process, communication between a teacher and a student is concerned with the transmission of a message either to increase a student's knowledge or to change his attitudes, his beliefs or his behaviour in some way.

Learning can be defined as *a process of acquiring knowledge or changing attitudes, behaviour or beliefs by contact with external events.* The purpose of formulating learning theories is to give a deeper understanding of the process of learning, but whereas in the past psychologists based their consideration of the communication which must exist between the teacher and the learner in terms of stimulus and response without regard to the human organisms involved, recent interest has centred more on the individual and the variety of motives, stimulations and functions that modify his reception of the message.

In this chapter we shall explore briefly theories of learning which are concerned with stimulus/response interactions, principally the work of Watson, Thorndyke and Skinner. We shall discuss work concerned with the student as an active processor of information and consider what practical principles of learning can be applied in order to help in the design of course materials.

Stimulus/Response Theories

In 1913, John Watson (1878-1958) published a paper, 'Psychology as the Behaviourist Views It'. As the father of the behaviourist movement, Watson was not interested in the inner self of the person but only in how thought and emotion showed itself in behaviour. He was concerned with reducing complex behaviour to simpler stimulus/response units so that learning which occurred at the level of these simple units could then be built into complex repertoires of behaviour.

As an extension of this he was also concerned with the principles of 'frequency' and 'recency'. The more often we make a given response to a given stimulus the more likely we are to make that response again is the notion which lies behind the 'frequency' principle. The principle of 'recency' is that the more recently we have made a particular response to a stimulus the more likely we are to make that response again. Although Watson's ideas were never carried through to reach clear explanations, he made a contribution to psychology in his emphasis on the study of observable behaviour, thus paving the way for later behaviourists.

Edward Thorndyke (1874-1949) based his view of learning not simply on the strengthening effect of the stimulus and response occurring together but more on the effects following the response. He formulated the 'law of effect' which states that strengthening of the stimulus/response bonds occur when followed by satisfying conditions, i.e. something in the nature of reinforcement by reward for good behaviour.

The Importance of Reinforcement

B.F. Skinner (b.1904) has long been concerned specifically with reinforcement as a basic factor in learning. With regard to Watson's principles of 'frequency' and 'recency', which he considers as the theory of 'learning by doing', he proposes that rather than learning occurring by the principle of 'frequency' as defined above, it is the frequent drill practice that enables our students to remember a particular response. The principle of 'recency' he considers occurs under favourable conditions, i.e. the conditions reinforce the response.

He reduces traditional ways of characterising teaching and learning to learning by doing, learning from experience, learning by trial and error. He dismisses these theories in the following words: 'such theories are now of historical interest only . . . We may turn instead to a more adequate analysis of the changes which take place as a student learns.' (Skinner, 1968.)

Skinner's 'more adequate analysis' is concerned with what he referred to as 'operant behaviour'. He suggests that whereas certain behaviour is elicited by specific stimuli, operant behaviour is emitted by the organism itself. He considers that most behaviour is of this kind, e.g. talking, eating, walking etc. His concern was thus not with the stimulus/response connections but with the ways in which operant behaviour could be brought under control and subject to modification.

Skinner's best known article which has a special bearing on teaching and learning as communication is 'The Science of Learning and the Art of Teaching', originally read at a conference at the University of Pittsburgh in March 1954 (Skinner, 1968). In it he describes briefly his work on the shaping of the behaviour of pigeons and goes on to apply his ideas to the teaching and learning process with students. He is particularly critical of the relative infrequency and delay in reinforcement of material presented to and produced by students. This article describes primarily the programme of work pursued at Harvard under his guidance. The results of this work are reported in 'Teaching Machines' (Skinner, 1968).

In this latter article he defines the teaching situation as follows: 'A student is "taught" in the sense that he is induced to engage in new forms of behaviour.' He mentions that in order to do this there has to be some form of 'teaching machine', thus producing a situation akin to that of having a private tutor who insists on material being understood before the student is allowed to move on while allowing the student to work at his own pace.

This communication of information by what is basically a linear question and answer sequence has become part of what is now known as the programmed learning movement. Although there are a number of other names and a variety of intricacies associated with the programmed learning of the 1960s, we shall not pursue them here. For those who would like to continue this topic the booklet by Leith, *Second Thoughts on Programmed Learning* (Leith, 1969), should prove useful.

The importance of the programmed learning movement here lies in the practical principles for learning that emerged from the work of Skinner and others. These were concerned with motivation, activity, reinforcement, limits on the amount and complexity of material presented etc. These practical learning principles will be taken up again later in this chapter.

So far we have been concerned with learning theories which consider that complex behaviour patterns are capable of being broken down into simple units where stimulus to the organism, response from the organism, and conditions under which these occur are the important variables. The use of the impersonal word 'organism' serves to show what little regard these learning theories had for the recipient of the stimulus and for the inner workings of the organism necessary to produce a response.

The Gestalt psychologists attempted to redress this balance since they were concerned not simply with the mechanistic aspects of behaviour and the connections between them, but also with the way in which an organism interpreted and perceived stimuli presented to it as a unified whole.

Insightful Learning

The Gestalt movement (the German word *Gestalt* means 'form' or 'pattern') was started by the German psychologist Max Wertheimer (1880-1943). Whereas Gestalt psychologists concentrated mainly on the way in which the organism restructured the stimuli presented to it and this depended on the way in which they were perceived, Kurt Lewin (1890-1947) took this concept further. He was concerned with aspects of motivation, needs, personality etc. Lewin's 'field theory' of learning was concerned with how a learner gains insight into himself and the things around him and how he then uses these to react to events around him. Perhaps the most important contribution made to the understanding of learning was the concept of 'insight'. Insightful learning occurs when one suddenly feels that one really understands or, as my mathematics teacher used to say, when 'the penny had finally dropped'.

Practical Learning Principles

Although there is now an increasing concern with the way students process information, until recently very few general principles have existed that can be distilled from the type of learning theories discussed above which give guidance in designing practical learning situations. However, there have been a variety of attempts, e.g. Bugelski (1956), to propose such general principles, including those which have arisen from the programmed learning movement (Hills, 1966).

Bugelski's attempt was derived from work by Thorpe and Schmuller (1954) which had examined leading learning theories for such practical learning principles. From this work he proposed the following five general principles:

1. Learning proceeds most effectively and tends to be most permanent when the learner is motivated, that is, when he has a stake, as it were, in the activity being undertaken.
2. Learning proceeds most rapidly and tends to be most permanent when the activity involved is geared to the learner's physical and intellectual ability to perform that activity.
3. Learning proceeds most effectively and tends to be most permanent when the learner is provided with the opportunity of perceiving meaningful relationships among the elements of the goal towards which he is working.
4. Learning goes forward with relatively greater effectiveness when the learner is provided with some criterion for indicating specifically what progress he is making.
5. Learning is facilitated when it goes forward under conditions in which the learner also experiences satisfactory personality adjustment and social growth.

It is interesting to note that all of these principles are concerned with the internal processes of the learner, namely,

1. motivation of the learner
2. the physical and intellectual ability of the learner
3. the need for perception of meaningful relationships by the learner
4. the need for feedback on his progress
5. the experiencing of satisfactory personality adjustment and social growth by the learner.

These principles contain a mixture of factors most of which are capable of being manipulated directly by the teacher in designing communications with his students. An example of this is the need to provide feedback on progress. Other principles however like maturation can only be taken account of by the teacher; he has little or no control over them. The second principle given 'when the activity involved is geared to the learner's physical and intellectual ability' is an example of this.

In this section I shall be concerned only with four of the factors over which the teacher does have control and where the design of communications or the framework in which it is presented can affect the reception of the message. These factors can be expressed in terms of the following key words: *motivation, activity, understanding, and feedback.* Let us consider each of these in turn.

Motivation

Motivation is concerned both with factors of arousal of interest and with maintenance of that interest. Since curiosity is thought to be a natural trait in human beings, interest should be aroused if some novel stimulus is presented; conversely interest will be diminished if a task becomes repetitive or boring. This is often the experience of a lecturer when his interest wanes in a subject because he has to give the same lecture time after time. If, however, the presentation can be varied or new material introduced, all the interest and enthusiasm for the subject revives.

Arousal of interest can be seen very clearly in young children because everything is a novel experience and therefore new stimuli are constantly being presented. The experience of teachers in junior schools is that in many instances once a child's interest has been aroused the challenge of exploring a new situation can occupy the child for long periods, often longer than an adult coming new to the same situation. This may be due to the adult's ability to relate a new situation to knowledge which he already possesses, thus shortening the period of time necessary to absorb the new information. This is a point which we shall take up again below.

The need for the arousal of interest thus argues for the need to present material in a way that not only engages the student in the task but which also, most importantly, contains elements of challenge. Further, although the arousal of interest may be sufficient to ensure maintenance of interest in young children, something more is required for adults. Apart from the need to design the material so that it continues to engage the interest of adults, this interest should be maintained by the teacher. This can often be achieved by keeping a feeling of personal contact apparent. The results of the well-known Hawthorn experiment support this. An experiment comparing external incentives with the development of a feeling of *esprit de corps* in the workers was conducted at the Hawthorn works of the Western Electric Company. The general result of this experiment appeared to be that external incentives had less effect on the work than that produced by better morale and the feeling that the management had a personal interest in each worker.

This personal interest in a student is, or should be, a normal factor in a schoolteacher's repertoire, but not necessarily in a lecturer's. This is due both to the freer atmosphere and the feeling that a lecturer is there only to lecture and to have little other contact with students. Thus with regard to motivation the two points which emerge most strongly for any teacher is the need to present material in a way that will both engage a student's interest and also maintain that interest by making the material stimulating and by making him feel that he is not being left to struggle with it completely on his own. The development and maintenance of group work and group feeling with other students can also contribute to this and will be dealt with in Chapter 6.

Activity

The principle of activity is a fairly obvious one, for without some level of activity in the student learning cannot take place. The most common picture presented of the lecture situation is that of the passive student and the active lecturer; the process should, however, be designed to turn towards inducing activity in the student. The need for activity was one of the central themes of the programmed learning movement where the assumption was that, by careful preplanning and testing, materials could be produced which maintained a level of activity in the student, making him work through material containing a sequence of questions and answers of increasing complexity. The problem was that these materials were restrictive, repetitive and often boring.

Present trends towards the individualisation of instruction as exemplified in the Postlethwaite Audio Tutorial approach, the Keller Plan and others (Hills, 1976) also build in these elements of activity by working with structured workbooks, practical work and a variety of media. What is most important with regard to activity however is the need to ensure that the student knows how to be active. Take for example the lecture situation described earlier. The fact that a student is, to all appearances, sitting passively in a lecture does not mean that his mind is not actively engaged by it. Chapter 8 will be particularly concerned with this problem when it considers the student as receiver. This chapter will look at the process in terms of a number of inputs of information to the student and how he can actively deal with these. In the case of the lecture the need for activity is stressed in terms of the difference between merely 'hearing' and actively 'listening' — a note-taking and questioning process is advocated. Chapter 8 also looks in detail at the processes within the student and the levels and types of activity that he needs to undertake.

Understanding

From the moment a child is born he begins to acquire information, to form concepts and ideas about the the world in which he lives. At first these will be limited to his immediate environment, but as his life expands he begins to learn things about his neighbourhood, his town, his country.

Each of us has built up a complex set of understandings about many things. These we can call 'frames of reference' as they are our internal models of the world about us. Whenever new information is presented to us we try to fit it into our existing understanding of things, to make it consistent with the frames of reference which we already hold. There is a tendency in terms of this to minimise inconsistencies between what we already know and what is presented to us. Read again the first sentence of this section — you may have already seen that the word 'the' appears twice in the first sentence, but then again you may not have noticed this. Our daily newspapers are full of this type of inconsistency, often because of faulty proof reading, but it is something we tend not to notice.

Some householders use this tendency we have of minimising incon-sistencies by putting up a notice outside their garage doors which reads

'Polite notice. No parking'. Usually, when someone sees this for the first time he misreads 'polite' as 'police', thus giving the notice more authority than it might otherwise have.

When a young child has new information or a new experience presented to him it can alter his behaviour drastically. However, this does not usually occur to such a great extent in adults since a frame of reference already exists into which the new information is incorporated. It is important for us as teachers to recognise that when we communicate new information to our students we should attempt to ensure that each student receiving it has a sufficient understanding of the background and context of the communication.

Feedback

Just as we should ensure that a student has a background knowledge of a subject before he goes further into the subject, so we ought to help him to continue to monitor his progress, giving him continued assurance that he is progressing or alternatively giving him help if he is failing to achieve his objectives. Bugelski expresses this as: 'Learning goes forward with relatively greater effectiveness when the learner is provided with some criterion for indicating specifically what progress he is making.' (Bugelski, 1956.)

This statement is somewhat at variance with the way in which students are for the most part given information by tests, by the comments and marks on an essay, and by end-of-term and end-of-year examinations. In these 'traditional' ways of providing feedback to students on their progress there is often a considerable delay in, for example, marking an essay and returning it to the student. The main point here, unfortunately, is that essays, tests and examinations have been thought of as tools of assessment for the teacher in order that he might see how the student is getting on, not for the student to monitor his own progress.

The possibility of feedback of information to the student on his progress is becoming increasingly recognised as individualised methods like the Keller Plan begin to be more widely known. In the Keller Plan the course is split up into units of material each of which contains a test of progress which the student takes at the end. This test is then marked by a tutor and discussed with the student immediately so that any problems can be sorted out.

The idea of feedback need not however be confined to individualised methods of education. It can and should be applied to all methods. In Hills (1976), I have already described work incorporating feedback which uses self-test questions as a support system to what was mainly a conventional first-year course consisting of a series of lectures. In this book I also describe work with a first-year course on chemical bonding which used booklets of basic information containing self-test questions for feedback with lectures given mainly as problem-solving sessions. These and other ways of keeping students informed of their progress are perfectly possible within the framework of any type of course; they also can carry the great advantage that the student has closer contact with the teacher. This helps to maintain motivation.

Current Trends

The work of educational psychologists like Bruner, Rogers, Perry and Pask all reflect the present concern with the student not as a passive recipient of a communication but as an active processor of information. Perry's work is particularly interesting in this connection because he gives nine possible stages of a student's development.

Position 1 is that in which the student sees the world in polar terms: 'Right Answers for everything exist in the Absolute, known to Authority whose role is to mediate [teach] them.' Positions 2 to 5 continue the stages through which the student perceives and accepts diversity of opinion until 'the student perceives all knowledge and values [including authority] as contextual and relativistic'. In Position 6 the student sees 'the necessity of orientating himself in a relativistic world'. Positions 7 to 9 involve the student in making a commitment in some area, exploring this commitment and finally realising 'commitment as an ongoing unfolding activity through which he expresses his life style' (Perry, 1970).

As these stages obviously affect the way in which the student perceives the world, they will also affect the way in which the student processes information.

This work, together with papers by the educational psychologists mentioned above and others, is reproduced in a book of readings, *How Students Learn* (Entwistle and Hounsell, 1975). This useful book contains, for example, an article by Daniel describing the work of Gordon Pask which includes his experiments on serialist and holist learners. The final chapter by Entwistle and Hounsell deals with 'How Students Learn: Implications for Teaching in Higher Education'. This, when taken with the other readings, provides a comprehensive view of the work of leading educational psychologists and current trends in the teaching/learning process.

It is possible and indeed highly probable that as more work is done on the ways in which students process information we shall begin to perceive how to structure and present material effectively to individual students. This represents a swing of concern in the communication process from the teacher's presenting material with little idea of how it is received by the student to a realisation that in learning it is the individual student who is important. In the absence of more definitive guidelines teachers should design their courses and subject material bearing in mind that motivation, activity, understanding and feedback, as described here, are all important active principles to help the student in his reception of the educational message.

4 VERBAL AND NON-VERBAL COMMUNICATION

In the next chapter we shall be discussing the form of communication which uses audio-visual materials; in this chapter however I want to concentrate on the teaching and learning process in terms of the verbal and non-verbal aspects of communication.

Verbal Communication

Sound carries information to our ears; from there this information is conveyed to our brain. Sound is the medium which is used by the voice to convey words to a listener, but it is the listener who transforms these words into meaning. If we adopt for a moment the restricted view that the verbal communication process can be represented as

Teacher talks ⟶ Student receives words

then the message can be passed by the teacher simply saying words and the student passively receiving them. There are however two important things to note in connection with this, one concerned with teacher-talk and the other with the student's reception of the message.

Teacher-talk

Teacher-talk is not merely using the voice to deliver words in a set way. In addition to the words spoken there are many possible differences in sound, tone, pitch, rhythm etc.

Sound intensity is measured in decibels. A quiet whisper heard at a distance of six feet may have a sound intensity of five decibels, whereas a pneumatic drill may have an intensity of one hundred decibels when heard from across the street. Between these two intensities there is the whole range of sounds, from very soft to very loud, to which our hearing responds. Over 100 decibels the intensity of sound begins to overload our hearing and can cause pain and possible damage as pop group performers and their fans have sometimes found out to their cost.

Hall in his book, *The Silent Language* has categorised speech in terms of distance between speaker and listeners, intensity of voice and content of the message (Hall, 1959). The following is an adaptation of four of his categories.

Content of message	Distance	Intensity of voice
personal or confidential talk	closer than 4 ft	whisper for confidential material
		soft voice for personal material
conversation between two people	4-6 ft	normal voice
information for anyone to hear	6-8 ft	normal voice perhaps slightly loud
lecture or public speaking	8-20 ft	loud voice

Like many things in the teaching/learning process this appears obvious when it is written down, but how often have we sat through a lecture where the lecturer's voice reaches only to the front row?

Loudness, like all other aspects of the voice, is a tool that can be used to enhance and improve verbal communication. A deliberately quiet voice at the beginning of a lecture can focus attention providing the speaker does it deliberately and then increases his volume when the audience's attention has been gained.

Similarly, tone and pitch can be varied and indeed are varied in ways of which we are often unaware since our voice largely reflects our inner state. If we are depressed, we generally talk slowly in a lower pitched than normal voice. If we are excited, we tend to speak more quickly and at a higher pitch.

The rhythm of our voice can be varied. We can vary speed of delivery, introduce hesitations, repetitions and silences. Rhythm is something that we think about more in terms of music where a recurrent pattern and a flow of combinations of sounds generally pleases us and may stimulate our emotions. A random pattern of sounds can disturb or irritate us. The voice, since it is an instrument and can be discordant or pleasing, should be thought of in these terms when students are subjected to large (or even small) doses of it — bearing in mind that a boring or soporific voice can easily lull one's listeners to sleep.

Speed of delivery is important since the student needs to have time to process the speaker's words. Normal rates of speaking vary from between about 100 to 200 words per minute. A slow distinct rate of delivery can have the consequences mentioned above, boring or sending to sleep one's listeners. In general, it is better to speak faster with clarity and introduce hesitations, repetitions or silences where appropriate rather than to speak deliberately slowly.

Many people are unaware of the way in which they do communicate with their voices. The point has already been mentioned that the voice can reflect inner feelings and emotions. Davitz, working with actors who were given the task of putting emotions into non-emotional spoken passages, found that many listeners could correctly identify emotions like admiration, joy, surprise, dislike, fear etc. (Davitz, 1964).

Listening to a tape recording of oneself can show these aspects. It is usually a surprise to hear oneself for the first time on a tape recording because, whereas other people hear you mainly by sound conduction through the air, we hear our own voices partly through air conduction and partly by bone conduction through the skull. Make a number of tape recordings of your voice — you can do this quite privately by using a simple audio-cassette recorder in the privacy of your own home — and you will begin to see the great variety of means of communication that is possible by using the voice alone.

Student Receives Words

So far we have concentrated on the teacher-talk; but what of the reception of the message? Before we proceed any further it is important to distinguish between 'hearing' and 'listening'. Hearing occurs when sound falls upon the ear; listening, however, involves more than this. It involves the processing of the message by the listener, and thus can be considered as involving the following processes:

Identification of words or sound

Relate to previous knowledge   Examine emotional or
and experience   other content

Interpret words or sound,
supplying any missing part

Think about what was heard
in personal terms

Sounds or words may only be heard indistinctly and thus the stage at which any missing parts are supplied by the listener is conditional on previous knowledge or experiences of the listener. This is why verbal communication can often be 'misheard'. Clarity of speech and planned repetitions of material may be important in this context.

In Chapter 3 we were concerned with how the frames of reference built up within the student and in what way these frames cause selection and distortion of parts of the message. When we hear someone talking we do not consciously realise the complex processing that we are performing in order to make sense of what is being said. As Rumelhart puts it, 'language understanding is an active process involving the interaction of sensory information with our general knowledge of the world.' In his book, *Introduction to Human Information Processing* (Rumelhart, 1977), he illustrates this at length in Chapter 3, 'Understanding Language'.

This also emphasises the importance of making sure that the student has sufficient background information to be able to listen. Someone who knows very little or nothing about the subject of a lecture will soon stop listening. There is a definite skill in listening; this involves making oneself interested in the material, something which can be done in a variety of ways. Adopting a questioning technique, as one does when reading a book critically, can help. Listening skills can be improved by any method which practises noticing or questioning things about what is being said. Students can be given simple exercises where they are told to listen for certain things in a spoken passage of material, after which they are tested to find out how many things they remember. The advice to a lecturer, 'say what you are going to say, say it, then say that you have said it', helps to direct initially the attention to the important things which are going to be said, and then at the end confirms that they were the important features.

Teacher/Student Interactions

So far the kind of verbal communication I have discussed has been of the restricted kind, but when we extend this to 'teacher-talk' and 'student-talk', that is, a question and answer discussion or even simply a conversation between two people, obviously the number of possible interactions is considerable. When a dialogue takes place people take it in turns to speak, and if the conversation is flowing easily there will be a definite rhythm of length of talk for each person, of the speed of reply, the tendency to interrupt etc.

When a conversation is not going well between a teacher and a student, or teacher and students, there is a great tendency for the teacher to go on talking so that the contact between them is not broken by awkward silences. This is done in the hope that it will encourage the student to speak and that once the rhythm of conversation has begun it will continue. Questioning can be used by teachers as a technique to draw responses from the students. Once set in motion the conversation can be shaped into a discussion covering the main points of the subject under consideration. The best way to get someone to talk is obviously to ask an open ended question, since one which merely requires a 'yes' or 'no' answer or a choice between alternative answers will effectively terminate the conversation.

The Choice of Words

Although in the above account I have concentrated not on the actual words pronounced but on the other communication possibilities of the voice, it is obviously important to consider also what is said, because the choice of words and their context can also carry meanings with them. Much of this area is summarised in what is still a very readable book by Thouless, *Straight and Crooked Thinking*, originally published in 1930 but now available in an edition by Pan Books (Thouless, 1953). In it, Thouless deals with words that convey emotional meanings, prejudice, logical fallacies, difficulties of definition, facts, habits of thought, suggestion and analogy, plus 'thirty-eight dishonest tricks which are commonly used in argument with the methods of overcoming them' — who could wish for more?

Non-Verbal Communication

When someone speaks he moves his head, his hands, perhaps his whole body. These and other non-verbal signals can give emphasis and force to a spoken message and may often show more accurately what the person speaking really feels — especially if the non-verbal signal is in opposition to the spoken one. A simple example of this would be agreement where someone says 'yes' and nods his head to show his agreement. On the other hand, if people disagree but feel they must appear to agree, they may say 'yes' but at the same time shake their head in disagreement. In this latter example, the person speaking may be totally unaware that he is betraying his true feelings by a non-verbal signal. The general emotional state of a person is often signalled by the tense or relaxed way in which that person holds himself. As with aspects of speech other than the awareness of the words spoken, teachers are often totally unaware of the non-verbal component of their communications. This is an important point which we shall develop later. Before doing this however I should like to consider some of the main components of non-verbal behaviour.

What is Communicated by Non-Verbal Behaviour?

There are three main areas:
1. to support or deny verbal communication
2. to take the place of verbal communication
3. to show emotions and attitudes.

Following the example already given let us consider head movements to illustrate these three. I have shown the first area in my earlier illustration.

The second can be illustrated by the use of the head nod as a reinforcement. Nodding the head as someone else is speaking serves as encouragement to continue. It thus has the effect of getting someone to talk more. However, if the listener begins to give a large number of small nods, it is probable that he will soon interrupt the speaker, wishing to speak himself.

Small, uncontrolled, jerky head movements can show that the person observed is in a tense state in which he is unable to control himself. This may occur when someone is in a state of rage. Generally, people who are relaxed will make steady, easy movements.

Eye contact is a particularly important non-verbal skill which should be considered by teachers, since it can close the interpersonal distance between them and their students. When one person looks at the eyes of another, a channel of communication opens between those two people alone. There is usually a heightening of awareness between them and the glances that pass between them can express friendship, love, curiosity or hate. Eye contact can be maintained for a long or short time, and can be maintained as an open gaze or a furtive glance. There are varieties and variations of these. A long, open gaze can indicate friendship or give reassurance. A long gaze may become a stare; this can also create anxiety by indicating aggression or dislike. On the other hand, a short glance may also indicate dislike or deception. If a person is anxious to avoid threats or being found out in some deception, he will generally avoid prolonged eye contact. Often, if a speaker is not looking at the person while speaking, he will make eye contact as he finishes speaking. By this means he is seeking information about how the message was received by the other person.

Eye contact is not the only possible variation here, because the eye can be narrowed, indicating that the receiver of the message is puzzled or perhaps afraid. The size of the pupil itself can change, e.g. his pupil enlarges when someone is looking at something which pleases him.

There are many variants and variations which can show non-verbal behaviour; these include those we have already mentioned, that is, voice variations, head movements, eye variations, as well as head and foot movements, nose and lip movements, posture, gait, hesitations and silences, touching, breathing, dress. To give some further examples, let us consider briefly these last two, breathing and dress.

Breathing varies with emotional state and is a good indicator of inner feelings. We tend to breathe faster when we are afraid, when we are in a difficult situation or when we are tensed up ready for action. We breathe more slowly when we are relaxed; when we are emotionally disturbed we may breathe heavily and yet be completely unaware of this.

Dress is another means of non-verbal communication that is often not considered and to this can be added the state of grooming of the person. Unkempt hair and a lack of care about dress may indicate a disturbed inner state of a person while someone neatly dressed with a well groomed look is probably well in control of himself. Overfussiness can, of course, indicate a tense, overcontrolled state. Generally, dress and grooming help us to see how a person regards himself or perhaps how he would like others to think of him.

The Teacher and Non-Verbal Communication

We have said that teachers think that they communicate mainly through verbal means, whereas in fact they also communicate many non-verbal messages to their students. If teachers are aware of the non-verbal components of their teaching behaviour, they tend to think that it is possible to learn and to control this. However, as we shall see from the last part of this chapter, although much work has been done in this area, a definitive taxonomy of non-verbal behaviours is not possible at this time. In the absence of this, the best advice that one can give to someone aspiring to investigate his own non-verbal behaviour is to read into the subject and to engage in self-observation. The use of video-cassette recorders with a television camera to record teaching behaviour can be very valuable in this connection; many universities, colleges and polytechnics now have such equipment.

It is important that the non-verbal component of teacher communication should complement and reinforce the verbal component. In addition the teacher should consider the non-verbal component to support and control the student depending on the desired circumstances. The following continuum is proposed by Victoria (1971) for non-verbal gestures in the teaching/learning situation ranging from those which are supportive to those which are unsupportive:

1. Enthusiastic/Openly Supportive. Qualities of unusual enthusiasm, warmth, encouragement or emotional support for students or situations.

2. Receptive/Helpful. Qualities of attentiveness, patience, willingness to listen, acceptance or approval; a responsiveness to students or situations implying receptiveness of expressed feelings, needs or problems.

3. Clarifying/Directive. Qualities of clarification, elaboration, direction or guidance.

4. Neutral. Qualities of little or no supportive or unsupportive effect.

5. Avoidance/Insecurity. Qualities of avoidance, insecurity, insensitivity, impatience, ignorance or disruption to students or situations.

6. Inattentive. Qualities of inattentiveness, preoccupation, apparent disinterest; an unwillingness to engage students or situations.

7. Disapproval. Qualities of disapproval, dissatisfaction, discouragement or negative overtones to students or situations.

As we have seen from earlier comments, one non-verbal gesture, depending on the circumstances prevailing, can mean one thing, but the same gesture taken in the context of other non-verbal behaviour can mean just the opposite. For example, eye contact can be supportive and friendly, but if it is prolonged and accompanied by a narrowing of the eyes, it can express disapproval. When attempting to analyse such behaviour, the basic point of all non-verbal communication is that each gesture cannot be considered in isolation. It must be considered both in the context of the situation and in the context of other related non-verbal components.

When a teacher is working with a large group of students, it is difficult to ensure that the attention of any one particular student is captured and held. Techniques of group work are considered in Chapter 6, but one of the points to bear in mind when working with groups is that the teacher should try to 'make contact' with each individual member. The teacher should attempt to make each student feel as if the work involves him personally. The obvious way of doing this is to ensure that the teacher speaks to each student and so makes direct contact.

However, this is not always possible in a large group and the use of non-verbal communication can be far more effective. Even with a large group a teacher can make individual contact with each student through eye contact. This individual contact can be repeated or used whenever the teacher considers it necessary. Students may go out of their way to avoid such contact by busying themselves sorting papers or taking notes. This avoidance of eye contact will occur particularly when students feel that they do not know the answer to a question and are afraid that they will be called upon to give an answer.

The area of non-verbal communication is one which yields valuable information to both student and teacher. Students seek non-verbal cues from the teacher as to the expectations of the teacher and the relative importance of the material being presented. This is why an understanding of the non-verbal component is so essential to the teacher; only in this way can he send out helpful and positive messages which complement rather than interfere with the verbal component.

By the same token the teacher can receive much information from how the students are reacting to the material he is presenting. If a student is sitting with focused attention then he is probably attending to and following the material presented. If, on the other hand, he is gazing out of the window or whispering with another student he may well have lost the thread of the argument.

Of course, this latter point is obvious to any practised teacher, but the question arises concerning what ought to be done about it. Here we have the limitations of any large group method where the teacher is essentially delivering information to the group. Each student is an individual and will be receiving the information according to his own particular frames of reference. Some will lose track of the material, others will still be following it closely. Should the teacher stop and repeat some part if he realises some students are not following the argument or should he continue for the majority who are still with him? Only you yourself can judge this in the context of the group you are taking at any one time.

One final point concerning the teacher and non-verbal communication, somewhat unrelated to non-verbal communication through gesture etc., is the need to consider the learning environment in communication terms. The old school classroom is probably the one which will bring back memories and can therefore be best used to illustrate the point. This often consisted (and still consists) of a room painted in drab colours with unplanned lighting and acoustic qualities, seats often arranged in rows before the teacher's desk set on a dais at the front of the room. The consideration of environmental space as communication is an important part not only of our formal education system, but of our lives in general.

Categories of Non-verbal Sample Teacher Behaviours

Love and Roderick (1971) have developed a set of categories with which to record the non-verbal behaviour of teachers in elementary and secondary school. It is reproduced here because it is applicable to many teaching situations and gives a useful indication of the sort of non-verbal behaviour that will act as communication to the student.

1. Accepts student behaviour
   Smiles, affirmatively shakes head, pats on the back, winks, places hand on shoulder or head.
2. Praises student behaviour
   Places index finger and thumb together, claps, raises eyebrows and smiles, nods head affirmatively and smiles.
3. Displays student ideas
   Writes comments on board, puts students' work on bulletin board, holds up papers, provides for non-verbal student demonstration.
4. Shows interest in student behaviour
   Establishes and maintains eye contact.
5. Moves to facilitate student-to-student interaction
   Physically moves into the position of group member, physically moves away from the group.
6. Gives directions to students
   Points with the hand, looks at specified area, employs pre-determined signal (such as raising hands for students to stand up), reinforces numerical aspects by showing that number of fingers, extends arms forward and beckons with the hands, points to student for answers.
7. Shows authority toward students
   Frowns, stares, raises eyebrows, taps foot, rolls book on the desk, negatively shakes head, walks or looks away from the deviant, snaps fingers.
8. Focuses students' attention on important points
   Uses pointer, walks toward the person or object, taps on something, thrusts head forward, thrusts arm forward, employs a non-verbal movement with a verbal statement to give it emphasis.
9. Demonstrates and/or illustrates
   Performs a physical skill, manipulates materials and media, illustrates a verbal statement with a non-verbal action.
10. Ignores student behaviour

Lacks non-verbal response when one is ordinarily expected.

Research into Non-verbal Communication

Relatively little educational research has been done in this area, most work which has been done having been pursued since the 1950s. Main areas of work by researchers into aspects of non-verbal communication are mentioned here and references given so that anyone who wishes may pursue this further.

Birdwhistell (1952) has been particularly associated with the analysis of non-verbal behaviour; he uses a notational system which represents movements of the head, the mouth, the eyes etc., symbolically. He has also been concerned with movements, for example, of the head and eyes which accompany what he has called 'markers'. Speech markers occur when the fall in voice pitch suggests the end of a speech or when a rise in pitch suggests a question.

Another worker in this field, Scheflen (1964), has been concerned with body posture and positioning. He has noted that postures often consist of clusters of specific body movements, such as holding a particular body stance with the head held in one way for a few sentences of a conversation. The termination of one aspect of a conversation could lead to a further grouping of body movements which are held for a certain period of time.

Hall (1959), an anthropologist, has been concerned more with what he has called the study of 'proxemics'. This is concerned with the distance between people during communication. He has found that there are social norms for distancing, and also that there are considerable intercultural differences.

In the area of eye contact, Exline (1963) has been particularly active. He and co-workers have been concerned with investigating the relationship between eye contact and positive or negative attitudes between people and the relationship between verbal context and visual attention. Hodge (1971) summarises a variety of findings in the area of eye contact in his article, 'Interpersonal Classroom Communication through Eye Contact'. Another useful summary article is that by Dunning (1971) entitled 'Research in Non-verbal Communication'. An often quoted and readable book is that by Fast (1971) on *Body Language*, which contains a set of selected references to the main workers in this field.

5 AUDIO-VISUAL COMMUNICATION

Visual Communication: the Teacher's Viewpoint

The teacher's concern is to pass information to his students as clearly and accurately as he can. He does this by coding his ideas either into the symbols of written and spoken language or into pictorial symbols.

The point has already been made in Chapter 2 that these symbols are representations of events and not the events themselves. Thus, the effect on the student of, for example, seeing and feeling (and smelling) an elephant will be rather different from his receiving a verbal description of an elephant from his teacher. Which is more appropriate depends entirely on the purpose of the teaching.

The example of the elephant is often used to illustrate that 'one picture is worth a thousand words', since obviously a picture of an elephant can convey more accurate information in a shorter space of time than many words of description. However, if the teacher were concerned with explaining the drinking habits of the elephant, a film might be more appropriate. The elephant is a good example because, apart from being difficult to obtain on demand, it is really too big to go into the average lecture room.

Thus the teacher wishing to support mere verbal description with visual material is faced with a choice of using one or more of the following:

1. real objects and three-dimensional models
2. pictures and drawings
3. diagrams
4. graphs and charts.

1. Real Objects and Models

Allowing students to view real objects can be valuable, especially when they are set in their own environment. Our educational system is such, however, that it is difficult for students to go out from the classroom or lecture room very often. Hence, these things or some representation of them must come to the student.

Whereas real objects and events may be too large or too small or too difficult to bring to the students, three-dimensional models can be made to be of a convenient size.

2. *Pictures and Drawings*

Often a picture or drawing will be sufficient representation. A projected
35mm colour slide has the advantage over a model in that it can be
projected to a variety of sizes. Models are of a fixed size and are often
intended more for individual use than group viewing. If different
aspects of the object are required, several pictures can be prepared
showing the object from different angles.

Drawings have the advantage over photographs of real objects in that
they can be simplified so that they can focus attention on specific
areas or facets of the real thing. Drawings are however a further step
away from the real object if some feeling for this is desired.

3. *Diagrams*

The diagram is an even greater step away from reality, but it is extremely
useful in showing the way in which things work and the way in which
the parts of an object interrelate to make the whole. Diagrams are
capable of considerable simplification and are of great use in describing
complex operations by breaking them down into simpler units of
material.

4. *Graphs and Charts*

Graphs and charts are yet a further abstraction, but are particularly
useful to show selected values from tables of data, so that trends in the
data can be shown clearly. This point together with others relating to
the choice of textual and diagrammatic material will be taken up again
later in this chapter.

An additional factor which has not yet been mentioned is that
pictures, diagrams, charts and graphs can either be static or moving,
depending on the choice of media, e.g. by using 35mm slide projection
or 16mm ciné film projection. Advantages and disadvantages of these
two will be given later in the section on 'the equipment available'.

Visual Communication: the Student's Viewpoint

The well known Müller-Lyer illusion is shown below:

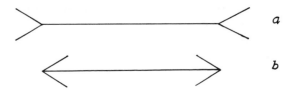

This consists of two horizontal lines of the same length. One line (a) has diverging arrowheads at each end of the line, the other (b) has converging arrowheads. To most people line (a) appears larger than line (b).

This serves to illustrate the point that what the teacher thinks he is communicating may not always be what is received by the student. There is not necessarily a straightforward one-to-one relationship between what the student receives and what he perceives. What he actually perceives will depend both on what he is directed to see by the teacher and also on the internal frame of reference to which he relates the image. This can be illustrated by a further optical illusion where what is seen is either two faces, or a vase or pedestal, depending on what you are directed to see.

A form of this illusion, together with countless other optical illusions and their possible explanations, are given in an excellent book by Tolansky (1964) if anyone should wish to explore this area further.

There are two levels of visual communication to be considered from the viewpoint of the student. The first is that discussed above where the teacher directs the student's attention to what the picture represents — the level of conscious appreciation. The second is the unconscious level where the visual material is being assimilated by the student but at the same time being subjected to inspection in the light of all the previous experience of that individual.

All visual information comes to us via the eyes, impinging on the retina and causing changes in the sensory cells. These changes in the form of electrical impulses are then carried to the brain where they are subject to some form of encoding process to preserve the information It is at this stage of encoding that the information is subject to possible modification through previous experience.

Carmichael *et al.* (1932) give details of an experiment where two groups of people were shown a series of simple drawings. As these

drawings were shown one group was given one set of descriptive names
and the other another set of names which could also have been applied
to the drawings. The groups were then asked to draw what they had
seen. In a very large number of cases the descriptive name actually
influenced the drawing. The people participating in the experiment
were being 'told' what they should see and were modifying their
perceptions in accordance with their previous experience of the objects
they thought they saw. For example, the stimulus drawing might be

the group given the name 'crescent moon' tending to reproduce it as

while the group given the name 'letter C' reproducing it as

(Abercrombie, 1960)

Visual Communication: the Equipment

No equipment is needed to show real objects and three-dimensional
models. However, unless the still pictures or visual symbols are shown
in the form of printed pages, some equipment, often quite expensive
is needed to display the visual image. There are a number of books
which describe this equipment in great detail (e.g. Dale, 1969;
Erickson, 1965). A useful short book is L.S. Powell, *A Guide to the Use
of Visual Aids* (1970).

The following lists some of the main types of equipment possible
for the display of visual images under four headings:
1. still visuals
2. moving visuals
3. combinations
4. data transmission systems and computers
   making points relevant to them in terms of communication.

To avoid lengthy descriptions at this point it is assumed that the
equipment is known to the reader. Should more information be

required any standard book on audio-visual equipment, including those listed above, should supply it.

1. *Still Visuals*

(a) Blackboard, various display boards, posters and wall charts. These have the advantage that they can be easily used to display either a small amount of information or a large amount of information. They can be used to show information for a short time or can be left set up so that the information can be studied over a longer period. These are not properly 'equipment' but have been included here for completeness and as a reference point.

(b) The overhead projector. This can be used for immediate use as a 'blackboard' substitute in a classroom situation, but its real advantage lies in its use with pre-prepared material. Transparencies can also be prepared which show a basic visual which can be built up by overlays to more complex displays.

(c) The 35mm slide projector. This can show any of the material used by the methods above, but 35mm slides require preparation (a 'write-on' slide is available but this is of limited application). One of its chief uses is to show good quality colour pictures of real objects. It can also be used to enlarge the very small or reduce the very large in size. It can project slides of any of the types of material mentioned in this chapter, that is, pictures, drawings, diagrams, graphs and charts.

2. *Moving Visuals*

(a) Ciné film. The type usually used for educational purposes is 8mm or 16mm. This can be used to project sequences of movement of real objects or it can be used for applications of (i) slow motion, e.g. to analyse an athlete's movements; (ii) high speed, e.g. to slow down fast events like the passage of a flame through a combustion tube; (iii) time-lapse photography to render visible movements that otherwise would occur too slowly to be observed, e.g. the opening of a flower; (iv) animation of diagrams, charts, or graphs to show an animated diagram of the circulation of the blood.

(b) Television. A television camera in conjunction with a video recorder can be used for the applications given above under ciné film. It suffers however from the disadvantage that the picture is not of the high resolution and quality that is possible with film. Additionally, educational establishments at the present time cannot afford the colour equipment so that the pictures are black and white.

3. *Combinations*

Combinations of media are now possible, e.g. slides and audio-tape, since the advent of tape-slide equipment. Ciné projectors and television are already in that sense combinations of sound and picture. There are now other combinations of media possible, such as the Philips PIP projector which combines sound with both still and moving pictures, and others, e.g. the Revox Audio Card, which combines colour microfiche with sound, although this latter is essentially like a tape-slide presentation.

4. *Data Transmission Systems and Computers*

This has been given a section on its own since it shows a new development in the direction of interactive visual material. Data transmission systems are being developed, for example, the Post Office's PRESTEL which can be used interactively to 'call up' a variety of data on a television screen. Trials of the system are only just being undertaken and its educational implications have not yet been fully investigated. At worst the system is capable of being used like the old teaching machines, at best the system is an information retrieval system capable of great flexibility. CEEFAX and ORACLE, the BBC and ITV data systems, can similarly display data on a television screen, but the viewer can only accept the images shown; unfortunately, they cannot be used interactively. PRESTEL is the relatively simple use of a computer over a large area by use of the normal telephone lines. Computers for educational purposes are already so used, e.g. for literature searches. Usually on a more limited and local scale, they are used for a variety of purposes which include (a) information retrieval; (b) the simulation of difficult experiments; (c) the manipulation of mathematical models; (d) problem solving and information giving of the usual computer-assisted learning type (Kornhauser, 1975).

Visual Communication: the Preparation of the Material

The teacher is concerned with passing information to his students as clearly and as accurately as he can so that the student may have the maximum chance of receiving it. The following account uses the categories which were listed earlier in the chapter, namely, real objects and models, pictures and drawings, diagrams, graphs and charts, and looks at some of the main points concerning the need for clarity and accuracy of representation.

Real Objects and Models. One is tempted to say that because a real object is a real object it is bound to present itself clearly and accurately. This, however, assumes that when viewing a real object the student knows what to look for. It is often desirable to prepare students for the real thing by showing them abstractions from reality, a diagram or a simplified drawing, so that their attention is drawn to important detail when they view the real object.

When showing real objects, one main concern is to ensure that they fulfil whatever educational purpose the teacher has in mind. If this is simply to ensure that the student is familiar with the object, either the real thing or an accurate reproduction will serve. If it is merely to show what the object looks like, a photograph might suffice.

Models can retain the complex detail of the original or can be simplified to focus attention on specific functions. They can be static or have moving parts, and can contain movable sections to allow inner details to be revealed.

Pictures and Drawings. A good photograph of an object can bring an inaccessible object into the lecture room. When real objects are photographed in their normal settings, care should be taken to use a viewpoint which gives a realistic impression. Distortion of the object should be avoided and it should be shown as clearly as possible without other non-essential objects cluttering up the picture. Where objects are small enough or can be removed from their setting, they can be photographed against a plain background.

Drawings have an advantage over photographs in that the viewpoint can be chosen and any unwanted material simply omitted when the drawing is made.

Diagrams, Graphs and Charts. Diagrams, graphs and charts should be clearly drawn. The example shown in Figure 5.1 shows a hand-drawn diagram that when photographed to make a 35mm slide will not be particularly legible.

In Figure 5.2 the same subject matter has been redrawn by a graphic artist. It is much clearer and has much more visual impact.

There are occasions, however, when such professionalism is not warranted. The graph shown in Figure 5.3, drawn by a graphic artist, gives added authority to the information presented.

Since the information contained on this graph is not established fact, a hand-drawn slide as shown in Figure 5.4 may be more appropriate in order to make the teaching point that this is a hypothesis.

Figure 5.1

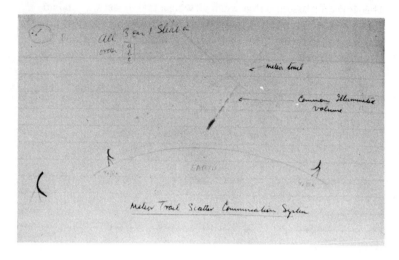

Figure 5.2

METEOR TRAIL SCATTER COMMUNICATION SYSTEM

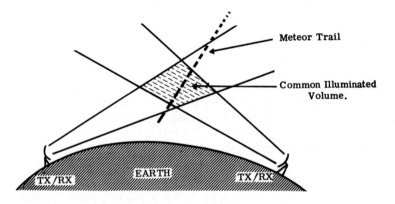

Figure 5.3

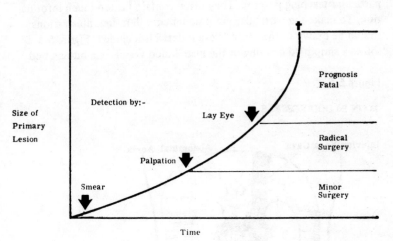

Size of
Primary
Lesion

Detection by:-

Lay Eye

Palpation

Smear

Prognosis
Fatal

Radical
Surgery

Minor
Surgery

Time

Figure 5.4

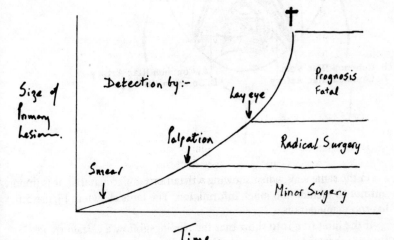

Size of
Primary
Lesion.

Detection by:-

Lay eye

Palpation

Smear

Prognosis
Fatal

Radical Surgery

Minor Sugery

Time.

Illustrations taken from books may not always be appropriate for a particular teaching purpose. They often contain far too much information. To make the particular point under consideration, illustrations should be drawn so that only relevant detail is included. Figure 5.5 shows a simplified drawing of the main blood vessels in a human body.

Figure 5.5

MAIN BLOOD VESSELS

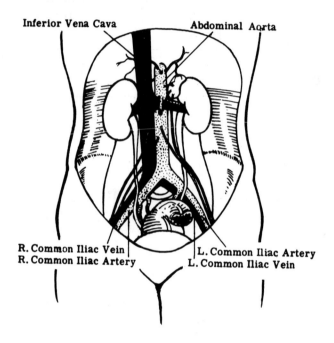

Inferior Vena Cava   Abdominal Aorta

R. Common Iliac Vein   L. Common Iliac Artery
R. Common Iliac Artery   L. Common Iliac Vein

In the same way, when showing written or tabular material, it is important not to include too much information. The table shown in Figure 5.6 has too many details.

If the intention is to show that the readings follow a certain trend, then it is better to use selected volumes as in the example in Figure 5.7. In this way the eye is not involved in a mass of unnecessary detail.

Even better, the trend can be shown in the form of a graph, as the example in Figure 5.8 shows.

To summarise, visual illustrations should be clear and carefully drawn. They should be relevant to the point which is being made. No

Figure 5.6

Relative luminous efficiency —scotopic vision

λ(mμ)	V′λ	λ(mμ)	V′λ	λ(mμ)	V′λ
380	0·000589	515	0·975	650	0·000677
385	0·001108	520	0·935	655	0·000459
390	0·002209	525	0·880	660	0·0003129
395	0·00453	530	0·811	665	0·0002146
400	0·00929	535	0·733	670	0·0001480
405	0·01852	540	0·650	675	0·0001026
410	0·03484	545	0·564	680	0·0000715
415	0·0604	550	0·481	685	0·0000501
420	0·0966	555	0·402	690	0·00003533
425	0·1436	560	0·3288	695	0·00002501
430	0·1998	565	0·2639	700	0·00001780
435	0·2625	570	0·2076	705	0·00001273
440	0·3281	575	0·1602	710	0·00000914
445	0·3931	580	0·1212	715	0·00000660
450	0·455	585	0·0899	720	0·00000478
455	0·513	590	0·0655	725	0·000003482
460	0·567	595	0·0469	730	0·000002546
465	0·620	600	0·03315	735	0·000001870
470	0·676	605	0·02312	740	0·000001379
475	0·734	610	0·01593	745	0·000001022
480	0·793	615	0·01088	750	0·000000760
485	0·851	620	0·00737	755	0·000000567
490	0·904	625	0·00497	760	0·000000425
495	0·949	630	0·003335	765	0·0000003196
500	0·982	635	0·002235	770	0·0000002413
505	0·998	640	0·001497	775	0·0000001829
510	0·997	645	0·001005	780	0·0000001390

Figure 5.7

RELATIVE LUMINOUS EFFICIENCY
Scotopic Vision

λ(mμ)	V′λ
400	0.00929
450	0.455
500	0.982
550	0.481
600	0.03315
650	0.000677
700	0.00001780

Figure 5.8

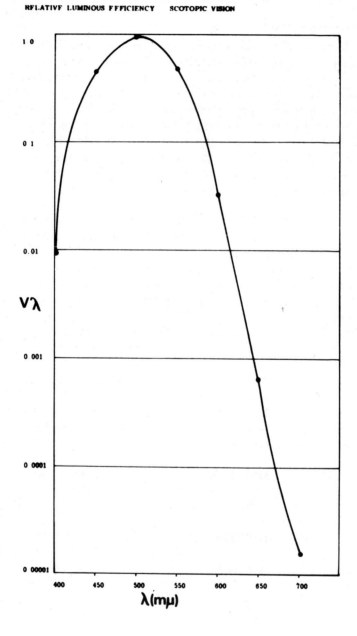

RELATIVE LUMINOUS EFFICIENCY   SCOTOPIC VISION

unnecessary information should be included. It is very important to avoid putting too much information into one picture.

Audio-Communication

So far in this chapter we have concentrated on visual communication, but obviously audio-visual communication takes place every time a teacher speaks to his students, writes on the blackboard or shows a set of slides. Increasingly however, as we have seen in Chapter 2, the teacher is making use of pre-prepared material to help his teaching or for use in small group work or individual self-teaching situations. In these situations the audio part of the audio-visual material is often supplied by a tape recording, using audio-cassette tape recorders which are relatively cheap and convenient to use in many teaching/ learning situations.

Audio-Communication: the Preparation of Material

The following notes indicate some of the main points with reference to preparing audio-tape recordings.

In the previous chapters under verbal communication we have seen how the voice is capable of variations in sound, tone and pitch. It is important when making a sound recording to use a clear, non-monotonous voice.

Although the intention may be to produce an audio-cassette version of the tape for final use, it is better to produce the original recording on a reel-to-reel tape recorder. This is important since it is almost impossible to record something without making at least one error. By using a reel-to-reel tape recorder one can edit the tape and cut out the errors. Editing a tape means simply physically cutting out errors and joining the tape together again, using a single tape-editing block and jointing tape.

Making a Master Recording. To make a master recording from which copies are to be made, there are special requirements in addition to those for a normal recording. The first requirement is low tape noise (hiss). The recording process introduces noise on the tape so that a tape copy has its own noise as well as the copied noise from the original. To minimise tape noise use a high tape speed, use high recorded volume and use the tape recommended by the machine manufacturer.

The second requirement is ease of editing. Mistakes and hesitations need to be cut out and occasionally corrections and pauses inserted. For ease of editing use a high tape speed, and record on one track only.

Common faults in recordings which affect intelligibility and the procedure for avoiding them are given in Table 5.1

Table 5.1

Fault	Avoidance Procedure
Tape noise (heard as hiss)	Use high tape speed, high recorded volume, and tape specified by machine manufacturer.
Hum	As for tape noise plus ensure recorder is earthed via mains lead. Keep microphone away from recorder. Avoid mechanical connection between microphone and recorder, e.g. both on same table.
Distortion (heard as roughness)	Do not record at too high a recording volume.
Inadequate treble (lack of brightness)	Clean tape guides and heads before use. Use high tape speed.
Poor acoustic balance (voice sounding distant)	Avoid placing microphone too far away, i.e. more than two feet.
Excessive sibilants	Avoid placing the microphone too near, i.e. less than one foot.

The rules for making a master recording may be summarised as follows.
1. Use highest speed available, preferably 7½in/sec.
2. Record in one direction only, i.e. one track per tape.
3. Ensure that the record level indicator shows maximum on the loudest sounds, but not more than this.
4. Keep the microphone as far from the recorder as is practical, i.e. at least three feet.
5. Rest the microphone on a cushion or hold it in the hand — do not lay it on the same table as the recorder.
6. Arrange the microphone-to-mouth distance to be between one and two feet, the final choice being made after trial.

The Selection of Audio-Visual Media

There has been much debate on what media to use in the teaching/learning situation. However, the main conclusions in the reviews of research, e.g. Kemp, 1971; Power, 1971; Hawkridge, 1973, seem neatly summarised by Kemp: 'The final decision on the most practical form to use should be an empirical one, based on any number of factors that need consideration.' As Hawkridge puts it in relation to Open

University policy: 'the University's selections of media are controlled by logistical, financial and internal political factors rather than by soundly based and clearly specified psychological and pedagogical considerations.'

There is at present no definitive guide to the selection and use of media. The soundest advice, in addition to the general principles of audio-visual communication presented in this chapter, is to use the simplest possible means consistent with a particular purpose. In many face-to-face teaching situations 'talk and chalk' can be supported by duplicated summary notes handed out to the students. These notes should contain main points, diagrams and formulas. In many varieties of group situations talk should be supported by duplicated notes. Where additional visual material is needed, the over-head projector, 35mm slides, video tape or ciné film can be used.

For self-teaching situations where the student is working on his own, directed references to a book or the use of printed notes may suffice. The audio-cassette recorder allied to printed notes is a reasonably cheap means of audio-visual communication to an individual student. A tape-slide presentation where an audio tape is accompanied by 35mm colour slides can extend the range of the communication but requires equipment and is more expensive.

When considering audio-visual media the kind of questions which must be asked are: Is there a need for additional audio or visual communication? What is the cheapest effective solution having regard to what is available in a particular situation?

6 INTERPERSONAL AND GROUP COMMUNICATION

The process of living in very great part consists of communicating with other people either singly or in large or small groups. Communicating with others is not simply a question of talking at them, for it involves an understanding of how they will receive your message.

To know others you first need to know yourself. How do you react to the communication of others? How do you react to other people? How do you feel when you are in a group? Are you at ease or tense? Only you know how you will answer these questions; you can with some certainty extrapolate from your answers the feelings which people have about your communications with them and the way they feel when they find themselves in contact with others. This is not to say that others will feel exactly as you feel, but rather that they have a range of possible feelings and reactions, some of which will be similar to your own.

Maslow has identified 13 characteristics associated with healthy people. These show the range of things to look for within ourselves and the characteristics that we can assume are present to some extent in those people we meet and communicate with. They are:

1. a superior perception of reality
2. an increased acceptance of self, of others and of nature
3. an increased spontaneity
4. an increased ability to focus on problems that are presented
5. an increased detachment and desire for privacy
6. an increased autonomy and resistance to indoctrination
7. a greater freshness of appreciation and richness of emotional reaction
8. a higher frequency of peak experiences
9. an increased identification with the human species
10. improved interpersonal relations
11. a more democratic character structure
12. a greatly increased creativeness
13. changes in value system.

Basically, someone who fits this description is a completely self-directed individual who accepts himself and others and is open to experience and ideas. How do you measure up to this? How do you think those people you meet measure up to it? How will the way in which characteristics of individuals differ affect the way they communicate to you and the way in which they receive your communications?

When people come together in groups they often quite naturally show anxieties to a greater or lesser extent, depending on the levels they have reached in the characteristics described. Argyle (1967) has described four main stages in group formation: forming, rebelling, norming, and co-operating.

Stages in Group Formation

Forming. First, few, if any, members of the group are probably known to each other, and there is the consequent anxiety of having to 'tune in' to other people and to find out how they will react one with another. Second, there is the task of the group itself. This may promote feelings of inadequacy in certain members of the group who feel unable to tackle the situation. There can also be anxiety about the ground rules of the situation and how the group is expected to operate.

When the group is forming, while people are finding out about each other and about the situation they are in, the individual members are subjected to a number of pressures and uncertainties. This leads on to the next stage.

Rebelling. If the group continues to meet, members will be getting to know each other, testing each other out. Some will try to adopt a leadership role, others the role of follower. Conflicts will be set up both between individual members and possibly between subgroups within the main group. There will also be a testing out and possibly a rebellion against the nature of the task and the rules of the group.

Norming. The third stage develops when group members begin to know each other and begin to accept each other and themselves in the roles they find most comfortable and acceptable to other members of the group. At this point the group forms an inner stability, conflicts are largely resolved and the group will come to have its own acceptable norms of behaviour.

Co-operating. With conflicts resolved, the group develops a cohesiveness and turns its co-ordinated energy to the solution of problems associated with the task in hand.

This is a largely idealised picture of the development of group co-operation; the continued stability of the group obviously depends on the maintenance of a variety of factors. Group satisfaction is one such factor.

Since the group has generally met for a specified purpose, the members of the group will continue to derive satisfaction only if they feel that the task is being achieved. One related point is how close members feel to the centre of activities. People on the edge of a group's activities often feel that they are getting little or no information on the workings of the group and that they have little say in its operation.

When the group develops cohesiveness, members are likely to be supportive of each other rather than in conflict and tend to reject threats to their existence from outside. In a cohesive group there is good communication between members and the role of the leader is important.

The Use of a Group as a Teaching/Learning Method

A formal lecture can be defined as a teacher standing in front of thirty or more students delivering what is largely an uninterrupted discourse for 30 minutes or more. In a group session, however, the teacher takes a much more subsidiary role. The main idea of group sessions is that the students should talk. Whereas communication in formal teaching is largely

in the group situation it is more

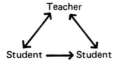

Group work is thus largely a means of encouraging discussion between students. Students should be able to say what they feel and think in groups so that they can share their ideas and ideals with others.

Used in this way group work is valuable for students in that they are able to see the way in which other people regard information and how they interpret it. This helps students to recognise that people differ in their reception of a communication and that there may be points for and against some course of action or argument which they had thought was clearcut. Being able to talk freely in a group also helps a student to put ideas into words and therefore to examine them in a more objective way.

Beal, Bohlen and Raudabaugh (1962) list seven characteristics of small group discussions.

1. They allow maximum interaction between members.
2. All members can participate.
3. Members are encouraged to think as a group.
4. Situations are set up which encourage leadership to emerge.
5. Members can broaden their viewpoints, gain understanding and crystallise their thinking.
6. They encourage members to listen carefully, to reflect, reason, participate and contribute.
7. They permit leadership responsibility to be shared.

Varieties of Group Methods

The normal group method, the tutorial, where a small group of students meet their tutor would seem the ideal vehicle to fulfil the characteristics listed above. In practice, however, students are often unwilling to expose their ignorance in front of the teacher, or indeed in front of fellow students. Often the students see no value in listening to someone else's opinion about something they think they know all about.

At the beginning of a tutorial, the typical question asked by a tutor is, 'Any questions?' which brings forth the usual silence. This then leads the tutor to take a topic of his own choosing and to give a short lecture on it. Teachers often fail to realise that there are other forms of group interaction which can be used to advantage. Students often fail to realise how valuable group discussions can be in terms of the characteristics listed above. As in all communications, someone should tell them. Bligh *et al.* has in fact listed a number of possible group interactions in his book *Teaching Students* (1975). These are given in summary on page 147, Fig. 5.5, 'A Hypothetical Continuum of Group Methods'.

The following account takes some of the main methods and discusses them briefly for the purpose of indicating firstly the diversity of group methods available for educational purposes and secondly the main purpose of each method.

Brainstorming. This is a small group method designed to produce creative ideas or a number of possible solutions to a problem. Members are instructed to express their ideas freely and in the initial stages not to be critical of any ideas produced. All ideas are written down and are later looked at critically. This method has the advantage that it can free students from the fear of expressing their ideas to others. This state often exists in the normal group discussion meeting.

Buzz Groups. This is a useful technique that can be employed between two people who happen to be sitting next to each other, or alternatively with a small group of people. Each person gives his thoughts on a particular topic to the other person or others in the group. In this way a quick informal exchange of ideas is brought about. Students can share ideas, exposing their thoughts in a non-threatening environment.

Case Study Discussions. As its name implies, the group is given a case study, which can be details of a real-life situation or problem or a simplified, possibly fictitious, study. The discussion of the material allows students to apply things learnt in other situations, to develop their critical faculties and powers of judgement; thus it can make them more aware of the complexities of human interactions.

Lecture Discussion. At the end of a lecture or lesson there is often a point where the teacher says, 'any questions?' This is an opportunity for the group, which has probably been subjected until that moment to the uninterrupted discourse of the teacher, to ask questions on the material presented. A good deal of the success of this depends on the relationship the lecturer has with his students. Students soon sense whether a lecturer can be communicated with in this way.

Tutorial. Here a small group of students meet a teacher for a discussion, usually without a central topic. This is in contrast to the seminar which is usually a group meeting to hear a short talk which is then discussed.

The tutorial is the traditional type of group discussion where, as in the lecture discussion given above, the teacher asks if there are any questions. Because of the anxiety of the students not to expose their ignorance before the teacher or their fellow students, nothing is said. The teacher then feels the need to fill what Broadley (1970) describes as 'the gap of silence', and begins to give a mini-lecture on a topic of his own choosing.

The tutorial should be the opportunity for free discussion and for interaction between student and student, and between student and teacher. Only when students have confidence in the teacher and are sure of the purpose of such a meeting and know and trust the other members of the group does this method work.

Individual Tutorials. Here we have the one student/one teacher interaction given under the Socratic method in the first chapter. It is often
quoted as the most desirable form of interaction because skilled
questioning by the teacher can build up complex sequences of learning.
The problem in using the method is that it is uneconomic in staff time
and in most cases, with even a small group of students on a course,
impossible to implement. However, using self-teaching techniques the
teacher can be freed from routine fact giving, and this may allow more
time for one-to-one interaction.

This type of interaction, except that it is between the student and a
computer terminal, is the subject of present educational research projects like those of the now completed National Development Programme in Computer-Assisted Learning. A summary of some of this
programme can be found in *Two Years On: The National Development Programme in Computer-Assisted Learning* (Hooper, 1975). In
addition to an individual tutorial-type interaction for normal subject
material, computers can be used for the simulation of difficult experiments or for the manipulation of mathematical models as mentioned
in a previous chapter.

Examples Classes. These are more formal than most group sessions. The
group usually meets to consider a number of questions or problems
which it is given. Firstly the students attempt to work through these
individually and then later they are discussed by the teacher. Another
form of this occurs where the teacher goes through an example and the
group then attempts to solve a similar problem.

Syndicate Groups. This can be used as an extension of the buzz group.
In this method a large group of perhaps 30 students is broken down
into a number of smaller groups. These are each charged with preparation of a summary of the main points of a topic which is under discussion by the whole group. One person acts as reporter, reporting the
findings of the small group to the whole. Points are recorded by the
teacher and then discussed. Buzz groups can thus generate the initial
points, but purpose and structure is given to the exercise through the
reporting back. These groups can be extended to include literature
searches and the preparation of more extensive papers by each of the
groups.

The Role of the Teacher in Group Work

The group methods described above have ranged from small groups without the presence of a teacher to groups where the teacher takes an active part in the normal tutorial.

The main role of the teacher in group work is to make sure that the purpose of the particular variety of group work chosen is fulfilled. In all methods the teacher should consider the need for encouraging the student to gain confidence in producing and exchanging ideas, seeking and giving help, and being constructive rather than destructive in his criticism.

The teacher should adopt a flexible role in groups in which he participates, taking the role mainly of listener to encourage students to talk, being directive only when necessary to steer the discussion back to the subject or to summarise the point made so that it can be recorded. The chief task of the teacher here is to encourage the students to produce their own ideas, to avoid correcting mistakes unless they are very bad ones, and to avoid dominating the discussion with what are obviously 'teacher' opinions. One should remember that each student will have some information relevant to the topic under discussion and one of the objects of group work is to persuade him to express this to the group and to himself.

Teachers often use three basic styles with groups of students: the authoritarian approach, the democratic approach and the non-directive method. The authoritarian approach is the traditional teacher role where the teacher is the fount of all knowledge and dictates all procedures and methods to the students. The democratic approach attempts to provide opportunities for students to think, act, and talk for themselves, growing towards the goal of self-direction. In the non-directive method the teacher tries not to let himself be looked on as giving direction to the group but listens and tries to interpret the group's own ideas and feelings back to it. In this method the group assumes its own responsibility for achieving the task it has been set.

In a group discussion where the teacher is assuming a directive role there are three main responsibilities he has to assume: first, starting the discussion, second, maintaining it and third, closing it. The following summarises some of the main factors concerned in these three stages in terms of teacher actions.

Summary of the Teacher's Role: Goals and Techniques of Discussion Leadership

1. Starting the discussion. State the purpose of the discussion identifying the important issues involved.

2. Maintaining the discussion. Make sure that members of the group focus on the problem in hand, analysing it and looking as it from various angles. Try to ensure that several solutions are proposed before they are examined critically. Provide summaries of progress made at intervals. Encourage the group to look critically at their solutions to the problem.

3. Closing the discussion. The issues and solutions discussed by the group should be summarised. Feed back information to the group on progress made to show members what they have accomplished. Set the scene for any further meetings.

In this account of groups, I have concentrated mainly on the process of group action and on the teacher's role within this. There are many factors of verbal and non-verbal communication which contribute to group interactions. Many of the major factors have already been dealt with in Chapter 4 and obviously these contribute to the conflicts or friendships between group members. Groups also have the curious property already mentioned of banding together against a common foe. When this happens the non-verbal signals even between members who have previously been antagonists become positive and supportive. In this connection it is important that the teacher is not seen as the common foe if he is to use the main purpose of group communication to the full, i.e. to encourage students to speak out and to examine critically their own and other ideas.

7 VARIETIES OF MASS COMMUNICATION

The formal educational system contributes only a very small part of the total amount of communication to which we are subjected in our daily lives. Our information is supplied, our attitudes, beliefs and opinions are shaped by a variety of communications to which we are exposed from the moment we get up in the morning to the moment when we go to bed at night. Chief among the mass communication influences we can consider newspapers, books, radio, television, film and advertising.

In Chapter 6 we were concerned with interpersonal, that is, face-to-face communication, and it is useful to contrast the main features of such communication with those of mass communication systems. The main differences are:

1. Face-to-face communication is a two-way exchange of information. Mass communication systems give a one-way flow of information.
2. Face-to-face communication can alter our attitudes, beliefs and opinions. Mass communication systems are largely concerned with entertainment and with knowledge dissemination.

This does not mean that mass communication cannot help to shape our attitudes and beliefs since the information it displays can help us to keep in touch with the events of the world, enables us to see all sides of important issues and helps to transmit the culture and values of our society to new members.

Messages from mass communication systems tend to appear in regular units of material, e.g. daily newspapers, weekly or monthly magazines, weekly television programmes. Thus if a particular communication, such as a daily newspaper, always carries the same slant on the news, the same cultural biases, through regular exposure then there may be a cumulative effect on its audience. This is in accord with Watson's principle of frequency mentioned in Chapter 3 according to which the more often someone makes a given response to a stimulus, the more likely he is to make it again. The mass communication media may thus shape our attitudes or opinions if we are exposed to them over a period of time.

It is appropriate to cite here the law of frequency because the original views of the effect of mass communication systems were that they operated in accord with stimulus/response theories of learning, i.e. messages passed across mass communication systems were the stimuli and produced responses in their mass audiences. This is very much akin to the lecture; there, one message is disseminated to a large group of students without regard to individual differences. However, just as students are individuals, so all members of a mass audience are individuals with different needs, different backgrounds and different perceptions. Designers of the messages for mass communication systems are now very well aware of this, particularly those involved in preparing advertising material.

Before we continue, let us briefly survey the main types of mass communication systems in order to set these in context.

Newspapers

Johannes Gutenberg was a German craftsman who invented a method of printing movable type in the middle of the fifteenth century. This is generally heralded as the beginning of mass communication, but it was only with the advent of Koenig and Bauer's steam driven circular press which was used for the first time by *The Times* of London in 1814 that newspapers really began to be agents of mass communication. At that time the press was capable of a speed of 1,100 sheets per hour. By 1865, Bullock's roll-fed rotary press was available and this could produce 12,000 completed newspapers per hour. This speed has now been trebled by modern presses.

In addition to the improvements made in the speed of production, there have been improvements made in many of the printing and production processes associated with newspapers. Today, newsprint can be set by computer and stories can be copy-edited directly on to the computer using electric typewriters. Type-setting over a distance, even via satellite, is used daily. The development of a series of news agencies, telex and teleprinter links has made news and pictures from all corners of the world instantly accessible to even the smallest local newspaper. As to the contents of the daily newspaper, these are compounded of a mixture of advertising material, news, feature articles, leader articles, pictures, letters and a variety of other smaller items like competitions and crossword puzzles.

Magazines should also be considered with newspapers. Although they do not contain current news, since they usually appear at weekly or monthly intervals, they contain much more information on special-ised topics. Indeed, the trend in magazines has been away from those of general interest to a wide selection of the public and towards the specialist magazine which carries informative articles on one main topic,

e.g. *Coins and Medals* or *Motor Racing*. This type of magazine carries
news articles which set the topic in the framework of the world's
events, or which report events involving aspects of the subject. The
direct educational content of such specialist magazines is often more
apparent than those of more general interest.

   As a means of mass communication, newspapers and magazines are
highly successful. Most people read a daily newspaper and there are a
wide variety of general and specialist magazines available. Although with
the advent of the Sunday newspaper colour supplements newspapers
have taken on some of the functions of magazines, it is reasonably true
to say that newspapers are primarily for news and magazines for entertainment and specialist information.

Radio

The British Broadcasting Company began broadcasting in 1922. However,
this private company was dissolved and replaced in 1927 by the British
Broadcasting Corporation as an independent public corporation. The
government had soon recognised the power of radio as a mass communication medium. Financed by licence fees, it broadcasts a mixture of
news, music and feature programmes. During the Second World War its
home and overseas news broadcasts were of immense value as accurate
sources of up-to-date information.

   The coming of television reduced the amount of radio listening,
especially in the evening. As a result of this, radio began to change its
image, experimenting with new programme forms, music and features
for minority interests.

   Since radio is a relatively low-cost medium, it has led to the development of local radio, which, like the local newspaper, has the ability to
respond to the needs of a smaller community. Local news, local
weather conditions can be combined with music and plays in such a
way that listeners can get a sense of belonging to a community.

   Initially, with the advent of television, radio was thought to be a
rapidly dying medium. Now, however, it is apparent that radio and
television can exist side by side, radio taking on one of the following
functions, depending on the programme listened to and the particular
needs of the listener at that time: giving news and information, acting
as musical accompaniment to a variety of moods, giving relief, com-
panionship and help.

Television

The British Broadcasting Corporation's first television service opened from Alexandra Palace in the 1930s. The service was closed down during the Second World War but was then reopened. The service derives its revenue from licence fees (there are over 14 million television licences in existence today). Commercial television was introduced in 1954 and derives its income from the sale of advertising time. In 1962, as a result of the report of the Royal Commission on Broadcasting, BBC2, the second non-commercial channel, was set up. High-definition 625-line transmissions were used and in 1967 colour transmissions were introduced.

At the moment, the situation is that there are three television channels all transmitting a variety of programmes, including news, features, quiz programmes, entertainment programmes, plays, a variety of special television series and repeats of old films. The emphasis is on entertainment value and not on educational value.

In this connection we must ignore neither the programmes especially produced for schools nor the Open University broadcasts. These are linked to specially produced printed materials and schemes of work. It might be thought that they should be looked at in terms of the appropriate selection and use of media for educational purposes, but Hawkridge's words are perhaps worth repeating here. 'The [Open] University's selection of media are controlled by logistical, financial and internal political factors rather than by soundly based and clearly specified psychological and pedagogical considerations.' (Hawkridge, 1973.)

Film

Since film and television perform basically the same function, i.e. presenting sound and pictures, film has largely changed from the vehicle for the epic production at the local cinema to the medium by which high-quality recordings can be made for use on television. It is obviously more convenient and less expensive to sit at home and watch television than to go out to the local cinema.

The decline of cinema audiences in this country since the advent of television is recorded by Williams (1976) as down from 32 million per week in 1946 to under three million per week in 1974. A corresponding decline in the number of cinemas is reported. The film industry has fought back to the best of its ability by experimenting with larger screens and more realistic sound, but the decline in audiences reflects the true picture, namely that of the need for more lavish and expensive productions to attract larger audiences. The industry has turned a considerable part of its output to the making of television films and series.

Film in its pure form is rather like the book in that, compared with the other mass communication systems we have been considering, these two are not regular events like a daily newspaper; they are not concerned with immediacy. Rather, they are concerned with painting a picture of an event on a broad canvas. They are akin to the play, but concerned with a wider audience. This is not the place to go into the techniques of writing material, although they carry a number of lessons for us as teachers. For anyone wishing to read further, I would recommend the book by Vale, *The Technique of Screenplay Writing* (1973) as a very readable book in this area.

Books

Books can be regarded almost as one of the first means of educational mass communication; most if not all of our courses depend in some way on textbooks, reference books or some form of printed materials. Books have the advantage over many of the media we have been discussing in that no equipment is needed to read them. Books, like slides, tape and film, give a record of events, but unlike most slides, tape and film systems, books can be skimmed through quickly, can be used for random access and can be used at times convenient to the reader for individual study.

The paperback revolution has meant that books are within the reach of anyone who cares to buy them. Television has helped the sales of many of the classics which are now often issued with a scene from the television series on the cover. The paperback revolution began in 1935 when Allen Lane published the first Penguin paperbacks. Now paperbacks can sell over a million copies of one book.

The relatively low price of paperback books in relation to those in hardback covers is occasioned by the use of high-speed, rotary presses, often using plastic plates photographed from the master copy rather than typeset in the conventional way. By becoming a mass communication medium, paperback books are sold in such large quantities that it is possible to keep the price down. Paperback books can be published in less than six months from receipt of manuscript to the books appearing on the bookstalls.

The educational possibilities of paperback books are considerable and some publishers print special student editions of popular textbooks. The ability to buy his or her own books is important to a student in order to build up a personal data bank, especially if the number of students on a course is great and only one copy of a particular recommended book is available from the library.

Advertising

Advertising I have left until last because it is all-pervasive. It shouts down to us from the hoardings and in the shops; it occupies much space in our newspapers and magazines and it tries to compete with the coffee breaks one can take during programmes on Independent Television. It is mass communication because it uses the mass media as a vehicle; its message is persuasion. As such it may contain useful pointers to the design of persuasive educational materials.

There are four basic conditions which must be fulfilled:

1. The advertising material must reach its audience.
2. The communication must be clear and correctly interpreted by the audience.
3. The audience should remember the main content of the communication.
4. The communication should be persuasive.

Cox (1964) sees the necessary conditions in terms of four key words — exposure, perception, retention and decision. These four words have strong implications for the teaching/learning process.

Exposure. 'Most people tend to expose themselves to communications in which they are interested or which they find congenial to their existing attitudes and to avoid communications that might be irritating or uninteresting or incompatable with their own opinions.'

Perception. People tend to 'misinterpret or distort a communication so that it will be more compatable with their own attitudes, habits or opinions'.

Retention. People tend to forget the content of a communication when it is not in accord with their own attitudes or beliefs. The converse should be true, i.e. people will remember a communication longer if it is compatable with their own attitudes.

Decision. 'Advertising works primarily by reinforcing or otherwise, acting upon people already predisposed to act.'

We see in these conditions the same sort of factors that concern the teacher in the teaching/learning process. It is interesting to note that practitioners of advertising still seem to regard it very much as an art, a mixture of words and pictures. There is a great concentration on techniques of layout and presentation as a look at the literature on this subject will show. The book by Bockus, *Advertising Graphics* (1969), is impressive not only for the range of techniques it embraces but also for the layout it uses to communicate these techniques.

Implications for Teaching and Learning

Mass communication systems are for the most part intended to provide entertainment and to assist in the selling of goods and services. Their educational value is secondary. However we have seen how they help us to keep in touch with the world and transmit the culture of a society to new members.

The news function of newspapers, radio and television is important in the educational context, but it is informational rather than anything else because like all mass communication systems they allow only a one-way flow of messages. The essential feature of the good teaching and learning situation is in the opportunity for feedback as we have seen in Chapter 2.

With the advent of audio-cassette recorders and video recorders it is now possible (subject to the necessary copyright restrictions) to record material from radio and television for later use. This overcomes one of the problems of this type of mass communication system in that it happens once and is not repeatable. Many ordinary television programmes have educational value, especially when used in the context of a particular course, e.g. wild life and travel programmes, although their primary purpose is to entertain. Many Open University programmes are also being used in more conventional courses with considerable success.

At present print as a mass communication system still scores over other systems in formal education because the skills of reading are developed throughout a student's school life. Courses in institutions are also largely print-based at present and hence it is to print that a student turns for information. Factors of ease of access to reference materials, the ability to reread passages and think about them at the student's own pace all contribute to the convenience of print.

Some people argue that this situation may not last because young people are now growing up familiar with television and, consequently, with an increased visual literacy. This may be so, but the nature of television is such that it transmits less information in a given time than it is possible to gain from access to a book. As an example let us consider television news in comparison with the same news available in a newspaper. Since most people can read faster than the newsreader is able to read the news out loud, reading a news story in a newspaper is quicker than watching the same story on television. However, it must also be remembered that television can extend the range of communication by providing coloured visual material and communicating non-verbal information on the topic in a way that the bald print statement can not.

Future Trends

Much of the media equipment that we now use in the teaching/learning situation was developed as a result of the spread of mass communications for entertainment purposes, e.g. the development of the ciné projector and television. There are indications that future developments in mass communication systems will influence the educational scene still further.

PRESTEL is one such system. As the system is developed much information will be available via telephone lines displayed on the ordinary television screen at the touch of a button. If, as is envisaged, local centres are set up to provide the necessary computer facilities, there are considerable implications for educational institutions on a local basis. The advantage of the system is that, unlike the similar television systems, CEEFAX and ORACLE, PRESTEL can be interrogated and information displayed as the viewer wishes not merely as it is made available in the television systems.

PRESTEL is a possibility that is with us now. Further developments in mass communication technology allied to computer developments may well lead to the concept of 'information utility' as described by Parker (1973). This concept may allow the transmission of material to be controlled more directly by the receiver of the message than has been possible previously.

It may look like a combination of a television set and a typewriter, function like a combination of a newspaper and a library, and permit a communication network that is something like a combination of a telephone and telegraph system . . . Receivers may thus select any particular communication (book, newspaper article, etc.) from a large storage medium at a time and place of the receiver's choosing. (Parker, 1973)

The consequences of the availability of such a system cannot be predicted, but, in view of recent developments towards individualised learning systems which often require a considerable bank of resource materials, the possibilities for individual study are considerable.

8 THE STUDENT AS RECEIVER

Although this book has regarded the student as more than merely the pas passive recipient of communications in the teaching/learning process, nevertheless it has not so far considered the process from the student's viewpoint. This chapter sets out to redress the balance.

Elsewhere I have argued that the long-term aim of our educational system is the development of the student as a self-directed individual and not merely as the recipient of a variety of knowledge (Hills, 1976). The student, however, sees his courses in more immediate terms. What lectures does he have to attend? What assignments does he have to complete? What can he do which will help him in the final examination? These are the kinds of questions that he is likely to ask. The 'student as receiver' end of the communication process may thus be seen as an input/output/processing model.

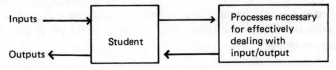

Inputs

The main inputs to the student on a particular course are usually:

(a) from the teacher in charge of the course on information about the timetable, the syllabus, various administrative arrangements etc.
(b) course content in the form of a series of lectures
(c) from the teacher and other students in discussion groups and other forms of group work
(d) directed reading given to the student from the teacher
(e) information from the teacher to the student on his performance concerning a piece of practical work, an essay or other assignment he has completed
(f) information received by the student on his performance in short tests or termly examinations
(g) informal inputs from other students which help to explain work to a student or give him some insight into the course which he might not otherwise have had
(h) reading done by the student either because he feels he lacks the

necessary background or wants to read further into or around a subject

(i) non-verbal information given largely unconsciously by the teacher.

Outputs

Outputs from the student can take the form of short verbal inter-changes with the teacher and other students, precis of written work or examinations, such as:

(a) questions or replies to questions by the student to the teacher or other students
(b) student giving a short presentation on a particular topic in front of a seminar group
(c) completing a written assignment, an essay, report, piece of practical work or handing in a set of completed problems
(d) completing a test or examination.

Processes Necessary for Dealing Effectively with Input

In a paper, 'Self-directed learning for 16-19-year olds', a colleague and I tried to identify the processes necessary for effective student functioning in this area (Potter and Hills, 1976). A version of the list in that paper is given below:

A student needs to:

(a) recognise and make the best use of teaching methods encountered
(b) recognise the value of learning strategies
(c) predict, plan and organise the use of his time
(d) know how to listen and to take notes from lectures
(e) create and use a personal 'data bank'
(f) know how to use libraries effectively
(g) know how to read books and take notes from them
(h) know how to prepare for examinations
(i) recognise and be able to use good spoken and written styles of communication
(j) adopt appropriate physical conditions for study including sensible eating and sufficient hours of sleep
(k) understand aspects of attention, concentration, perception, memory, personal work rhythms etc.

Details of the various inputs to the students are considered either in the next chapter, 'The Teacher as Sender', or in other chapters of this

book. As to the outputs which take the form of written or spoken
communication, the advice given in the chapters on verbal and on
audio-visual communication are all appropriate. Many 'how to study'
books exist which give detailed information in these areas. My own
book, *Study to Succeed* (Hills, 1973), attempts to do this by involving
the student actively in a series of practical exercises which lead him
through the methods of input and output.

Many of these study books are merely at the 'hints and tips' level,
and often this may be all the good student needs to brush up his
technique. However the average or not so good student may require
more positive help from his teacher because this type of student may
not possess the skills that are needed for him to gain the maximum
benefit from a 'how to study' book.

The following resumé briefly considers each of the eleven processes
listed and attempts to summarise their main points so that students
may be helped to think about them.

I believe this to be the most important feature of any advice that
students can be given to render the communication between the
teacher and the student more effective. Any student can be shown the
main features or ideas, but ultimately it is up to him to consider them in
his own terms and in relation to his existing and preferred methods of
working.

Recognise and Make the Best Use of Teaching Methods Encountered

Here the student will be concerned mainly with lecturer and group
processes. It is important for the student to recognise that the main
function of a lecture is to pass information from the teacher to the
student whereas group processes allow him to participate in discussion
and to hear other views on a subject.

A number of other teaching methods which often involve strategies
different from those of more traditional methods are increasingly
being made use of. An account of some of the main methods is given in
Hills (1976). Some, such as simulation and gaming which involve
active participation, have been well described by Tansey and Unwin
(1969). Others, involving computer interaction, are less widely known,
but a variety of applications are described in Hooper and Toye (1975).

As the next chapter emphasises, to ensure that the student is
familiar with the teaching methods encountered and can cope with
them, the teacher should make sure that students are given the necessary information. If this does not happen, however, the student should
always remember that he can ask the teacher.

Recognise the Value of Learning Strategies

This relates to all the other points which will be dealt with here. In essence, a student should recognise that he is not a passive recipient of information but that he can plan and apply strategies which will help him with the work.

The point made above about asking the teacher is a general learning strategy. If one does not understand or know about something, the appropriate person should be found and consulted. One must, however, be prepared either to get an answer which is not understood or no answer or to find that there is no simple answer.

This strategy of asking questions can be extended to the reading of books. If the student adopts a questioning attitude when reading a book, he will find that his attention is focused more clearly and critically on the material.

When preparing a piece of written material or preparing for an examination one useful strategy is to spend some time thinking about the main ideas and trying them in different combinations. This can be done by writing the ideas on cards or pieces of paper; these should then be spread out on a table in various combinations until one is found that seems most appropriate for the task in hand. This is a good revision method because it helps one to think about ideas in relation to one another.

Another strategy which can be very useful is that of working with others. If a student can find a congenial student or a small number of students, it is possible to form an informal group that meets to review and discuss the course work. This has the advantages of discussion groups mentioned in Chapter 6 but without the impediment that one might be afraid to speak out.

Effective learning strategies are generally those which enable a student to be in control of his learning situation, trying things out, and balancing his time, not simply being carried along with the work and often being overwhelmed by it.

Predict, Plan and Organise the Use of His Time

Following on from the last point, this should involve the student in taking a step backwards to survey the work load, the new life that he is leading and its principal features, and to try to reconcile his time pressure with the time available. This should involve making a weekly and a daily timetable of work, which should be used flexibly as a set of guidelines rather than a rigid taskmaster.

The advantage of organising time is that it can help to minimise counter-productive worry and indecision. By attempting to plan time to cover the known course requirements and by giving time to carry out any written assignments it should be possible to keep some time for relaxation. Another major advantage is that once time is set aside for a task all other things can (in theory) be dismissed and one can concentrate solely on the task in hand. Timetabling can also balance time so that difficult subjects are not neglected.

It should be stressed that students should work to a flexible time-table. The main advantage of this is that time available has been thought about in terms of tasks set. This means that decisions on varying the timetable can be based on knowledge of the situation and not on uninformed guesswork.

Know How to Listen and to Take Notes from Lectures

It is very possible for a student to apparently listen to something and yet be unable to remember anything about it. Listening, like most things about learning, demands active participation. Basically, listening is carried on in the mind. In order to engage the mind, it is first necessary to have the basic background knowledge demanded by the course; it should then be possible not only to hear the words said but also to let the mind 'play' with the ideas presented, questioning them, arguing or disagreeing with them and coming to conclusions about them.

Notetaking can help this process, but this depends on the style of the teacher. The teacher should write up on the board the main points of his lecture or hand out sheets of notes. Thus the student will have a basic framework on which to hang his notes, questions, ideas etc. Note-taking is usually thought of as a linear process, but some students find a 'patterning' approach useful where the main subject of a lecture is written in the middle of a page and other points and keywords filled into a two-dimensional pattern. Points can then be thought about and interrelated by joining them with arrows as the lecture proceeds. A detailed account of creative pattern structures can be found in *Use Your Head* (Buzan, 1974).

Create and Use a Personal 'Data Bank'

Many students just take notes from lectures and use these as a basis for their revision in the examination. Rather than perform at this minimum rate it is better for the student to adopt a policy of exploring subjects and building up a personal 'data bank' which will stand him in good stead during his courses and also act as a nucleus for future work. The basic realisation here is that at best a set of lecture notes represents only one teacher's viewpoint. By looking up the subject in one or, preferably, more books different viewpoints can be obtained. Notes taken from books can be used to supplement existing notes and also add additional points that can be used for written assignments or in examinations.

The two usual objections to this procedure are lack of time — an argument that can be countered if time is properly organised, and the possibility of confusion and lack of understanding if other books do not follow the exact course of the lectures. This latter is more difficult to deal with since it is often difficult for a student to reconcile different treatments of a subject with the one he has been given; this is an area where the teacher needs to give help and guidance.

Creating a personal 'data bank' is very like creating a scrapbook. One should keep one's eyes open for anything that has a bearing on work in hand and either note where to find it or write out short notes for inclusion in a filing system.

It is always useful at some stage to start a card index system. Filing cards, five inches by three inches, can be bought in packs of a hundred quite cheaply. A small filing box and set of alphabetical cards will be needed. Lecture notes, supplementary notes, copies of articles etc. can then be filed in any way desired, perhaps filed in sequence as received. Providing all cards are given a number they can be found easily and quickly by noting their details and reference number on an index card which is then filed alphabetically by subject. References to chapters in books available from the library can also be included in the card index. Figure 8.1 shows the layout that might be adopted.

Figure 8.1

Communication   Location —
                                                 own book shelf

P. J. Hills   1979

Teaching and Learning as a Communication Process
    Croom Helm Ltd. London.

Contains chapters on :
Human Communication and the Education Process

The details on this card illustrate one difficulty. It is sometimes difficult to decide under what subject to file the card. In this case it could have been either 'communication' or 'teaching'. With a large card-indexing system two cards would have been the answer, but with a small personal system one entry should suffice. Again if a card index refers mainly to books and articles on a subject it can be useful also to file a card under the author's name so that the information can be retrieved from this. Note that the card should also contain summary notes to enable one to see if the reference is relevant to the purpose without actually having to go to the full reference to decide.

Know How to Use Libraries Efficiently

The main sources of information to be found in a library are:

1. the catalogue
2. books on subjects kept on the ordinary shelves
3. books kept specially for short-term loan
4. books kept in a reference section
5. journals and periodicals.

Students should be encouraged to familiarise themselves with the location of all these, especially the location of books relevant to subjects under study. This is really all part of the process of building up a personal data bank. If they are familiar with where to find relevant information much time wasting can be avoided when the need to use material arises.

Library staff are usually only too happy to advise teachers and students on the facilities of their library. Students should be encouraged particularly to keep an eye on relevant journals and periodicals both for general interest and for specific references to their subject areas.

Know How to Read Books and Take Notes from Them

Many students believe that if they could take a course in rapid reading, most, if not all, of their troubles would be over. They do not realise that directed reading, i.e. reading with a purpose, is more important than scanning and possibly remembering a large mass of facts.

The following extract on how to approach a book to see if it will be helpful to you is taken from my book, *Study to Succeed* (Hills, 1973).

First, open the book at the preface in which the author generally states the scope of the book and his purpose in writing it. Often, if it is a textbook, he states the level and type of student at which it is aimed.

Next look at the contents page. Your first look at this gives you the main chapter headings showing the subject areas dealt with. If you were considering a plan of the book's structure, then the contents page gives you the broad framework, and your later investigations will give you the finer detail.

Now turn to the back of the book and skip quickly through the index. Where a familiar term meets your eye, look it up on the page given and see what the author has to say about it. If you are judging a book which is completely new to you, this is a useful test. With one or two topics which you know well you can see how the author tackles the subject. If his treatment is poor, then you should be cautious of his treatment of other topics.

In this preliminary survey you should go quickly through every page of the book, looking at sub-headings and chapter summaries where provided. It is possible to go through quite a large book in this way very quickly, not to learn or retain any of the subject material, but to see the author's intention, his broad organisation, and some of the finer detail. After doing this the book becomes familiar. It is no longer a strange thing designed to stay on a shelf in the hope that its mere possession will help you in your studies — it is something that can be used to help you to further your purpose.

The point is also made here that there are many reading speeds that can be employed from fast scanning to locate relevant material down to 'ordinary' speeds which are advocated for reading and learning technical material.

Notetaking from books has already been touched upon in terms of becoming involved with the material, questioning and thinking about the material. The technique is very like that involved in taking notes from lectures but with the added advantage that book material is more flexible. This can be read at a student's own speed, put down and picked up when desired, read and reread as necessary.

Know How to Prepare for Examinations

At the beginning of a course the final examination seems somewhat remote to students who traditionally try to cram their revision into the last few days before they take the examination. However, if students follow an organised plan of action, gathering data etc. as previously indicated, then they are preparing for the examination steadily throughout the course. It is often useful if the student prepares a set of summary notes containing an outline of the main points as the course progresses. This outline can then be used for revision purposes just before the examination.

Students should study old examination papers, going through questions, working out 'ideal' answers with others in the course. Adopting a steady approach to examination revision removes much of the last-minute anxiety, although it is natural that some anxiety will remain. If revision has been pursued steadily, the night before the examination should be taken off from work and the advice is 'early to bed'.

The following advice for 'on the day' is taken from *Effective Learning: A practical guide for students* (Haynes *et al.*, 1977).

1. Arrive early, properly equipped.
2. Check the instructions at the top of the paper, number of questions, time, and any compulsory questions.
3. Read the paper twice, taking at least five minutes.
4. On the second reading, make short notes against the questions you can answer.
5. Calculate the time for each question.
6. Choose your best question.
7. Answer questions in increasing order of difficulty.
8. *Always* answer the correct number of questions.
9. Answer the question asked, make sure you have covered all aspects in your answer.
10. Leave a little time to check your answer at the end.

Recognise and Be Able to Use Good Spoken and Written Styles of Communication

This involves some practice on the part of the student, but principally consists of advice and guidance from the teacher.

Adopt Appropriate Physical Conditions for Study

Getting enough sleep and enough suitable food are two essential factors. Eight hours' sleep a night is the usual recommended amount, but this obviously varies with individuals and the main thing is that the student should experiment until he finds how much sleep he needs. Food needs are equally variable among individuals, but sound advice is a 'good' breakfast and at least one decent meal a day. The main thing for a student to remember is not to try to save money by cutting down on food, especially fresh fruit.

When students are studying, they either work in their own rooms or in the library. They should be able to work with equal facility in either. Study in their own room has the advantage of a familiar environment, but the disadvantage of possible interruptions. Study in the library should be in an area near books in their required subject so that reference material is near at hand when required.

The need for timetabling, when working, is important so that practice in concentration on one task at a time enables a student once in a familiar environment for study to get down quickly to work ignoring all distractions — at least that is the theory; in reality it does actually improve with practice.

Understand Aspects of Attention, Concentration, Perception, Memory and Personal Rhythms

It is important that a student should relate these points to himself. This involves the need to realise that everyone has a personal frame of reference for a subject made up from a large number of personal experiences. Related to this is the need to have or to acquire a sufficient background knowledge of a subject to enable new facts, principles and ideas to be incorporated. Students should have the idea of short-term and long-term memory pointed out to them; this leads to the idea that rehearsal of facts either by writing them down or by thinking and talking about them causes the greater probability that the material will be retained in long-term memory. The actual mechanism of memory is still the subject of debate. A good pragmatic account, however, of the amount of information that can be processed by memory is Miller (1956),'The magical number seven, plus or minus two: some limits on our capacity for processing information.'

Concentration is focused attention. This concentration of attention applies to most processes. It is really attention to detail and this includes planning future actions, handing work in on time etc.

Personal work rhythms should be looked at by every student. Some people work better in the mornings, some in the afternoons, others in the evenings. Students should be encouraged to think about the time of day when they work best and arrange personal work schedules accordingly. Unfortunately, lectures, discussion groups and practical classes are largely fixed events, but work which a student does on his own should be considered in these terms and timetabled to fit personal preferences if possible.

This has of necessity been a very condensed account of the processes necessary for students to deal with the inputs and outputs of the educational communication processes. They naturally reflect my own frames of reference in this matter and, where thought necessary, the balance should be redressed or more detail added by reference to 'how to study' books. A number of these are listed in the bibliography.

9 THE TEACHER AS SENDER

If teaching were merely a matter of communicating the content of a course to a student without worrying too much about what happened at the student end, then the lecture might be considered to be an ideal and efficient way to do this. One lecturer stands up in front of a large group of students and communicates for an uninterrupted period of some thirty to fifty minutes. The lecture exposes the material to the student, getting through the syllabus reasonably quickly, and it is administratively convenient as a large number of students can be 'processed' by one lecturer in one room. However, the educational communication process is not for the convenience of the teacher: it should be for the benefit of the student.

In Chapter 8, we have been concerned with the student as receiver largely in terms of short-term aims, because these are the ones that the student sees and considers important. I have argued in *The Self-Teaching Process in Higher Education* (Hills, 1976) that it is important to help a student to learn not only while he is engaged in formal course work, but also to help him to become a self-directed individual. Mountford (1966) expresses the essence of this when he says we need to

> provide the student with a body of positive knowledge which enhances his store of learning and in part equips him for his career in later life . . . To the limits of his capacity he is trained to collect evidence for himself and form a balanced judgement about it. He fortifies his ability to think for himself.

Whatever techniques have to be developed in order that the student should achieve these aims ultimately depends on the individual student himself, and it is the task of the teacher to help him with this.

The teacher is not there simply to hand over the accumulated knowledge of the past, he is also there to help the student in any way necessary to try to ensure that he perceives a communication as clearly as possible and, to use the terminology of the model in Chapter 2, with the minimum of noise in the system. The noise in the system is not merely concerned with the passing of the message itself, but refers to noise in the total system. The system is the total educational environment that the student is existing and working in. This casts the teacher in the role of administrator and therapist, although perhaps the terms 'manager' and 'father figure' would seem less threatening to those who insist that their role is to 'teach'.

Teaching in schools has always seen the teacher in this wider role, expressed by Fleming in his book *Teaching: a Psychological Analysis* (1968). The teacher is 'a student of motivation . . . a promoter of learning . . . an observer of growth . . . craftsman and technician . . . administrator and therapist'. The requirements of this wider role has been usefully categorised in the Nuffield publication *Learning from Learners* (Parlett *et al.*, 1976) into four main problem areas:

1. inadequate exchange of information with students
2. the 'psychological barrier'
3. intellectual contact confined to formal teaching
4. scrutinising teaching and learning.

I shall adopt these headings to explore the four areas below, but I should like to begin with a fifth problem area which faces students when they transfer from school to an institution of higher education.

The Transition from School to University

In a way school can be considered an extension of the home. Students are largely supervised from the moment they arrive until the moment they leave. They are required to attend lessons, made to do their homework, the teacher acting as substitute guardian and parent, roles additional to those outlined by Fleming above.

When a student leaves the relatively protected atmosphere of the school for the freer environment of college, polytechnic or university he finds a very different situation. In addition to the academic course work, he has to cope with living on his own, probably for the first time, and facing the problems attendant upon mixing with a large number of people of his own age and beginning an entirely new social life.

Thus he begins his new life with an unfamiliar situation, probably with feelings of inadequacy and lack of confidence. He then quickly finds that the teachers appear to be concerned only with the content of the academic courses and that they expect him to possess already a multitude of what are probably to him new skills of notetaking, discussion techniques, ability to perform and write up practical work etc.

The task of the teacher is to help him to cope with this, to ease the transition, to help him until he can help himself. The remainder of this chapter explores the help that the teacher can and should give to the student, first in terms of the four problem areas mentioned above and second in terms of the inputs to the student and the outputs from the student mentioned in the previous chapter.

Inadequate Exchange of Information with Students

When students arrive, they need to know about the institution in which they are going to spend the next few years. They need to know about their own living accommodation, the facilities for living, social life and general student facilities. They need to know about their department, or departments if their work is split between more than one, and about the the staff of the department, especially those who will be teaching them. They must know about general working conditions, the library, details of course syllabuses, course and examination requirements.

All of these things are necessary to a student to help him to build frames of reference of the environment in which he works and to give him confidence to be able to cope with the very difficult world in which he finds himself. Most institutions now have a student induction course to which the student comes a few days before term starts; here he is talked at and deluged with 'helpful' pieces of paper. However, because of the conditions described, at that moment of arrival when he is probably at the maximum state of confusion he is least receptive and consequently may take in very little.

Many institutions now have the personal tutor system where students are given the name of a lecturer to whom they can go if they need personal help. Personal tutors are usually lecturers in the student's department who do not teach the students on their academic courses. This goes some way to help students to resolve their confusions, but one can run up against the psychological barrier described below.

Although to a large extent normal course teachers cannot help students with their personal living and social problems, every teacher should make sure that he gives students adequate information about a course, including a syllabus, required attendance at lectures, discussion groups and practical classes. They should ensure especially that students know how the course will be assessed, what form the examination will take, and how the marks will be proportioned.

This open approach will help to give the students confidence both in their course work and in their teachers. There are arguments against this, many of which defend the principle that students must believe that teachers know exactly what is happening in their courses and that all is fixed and immovable. This is often not the case and there would seem to be little justification for pretending that it is. To be able to adopt this open approach teachers have to work out what they are doing in advance and have thought about their course not only in terms of its contents but also in terms of the needs of the students. I believe this is the way in which the majority of teachers are now thinking, and it is to help them with those thoughts that this book is directed. There is however one very considerable problem and that is the 'psychological barrier'.

The 'Psychological Barrier'

Parlett *et al*. (1976) see this barrier as inevitable because of the stratification and the difference between the roles of teachers and students. They consider it to be built into 'the basic educational contract that exists between someone who has knowledge and someone who does not'.

Teachers often consider that no barrier exists, because most are always ready to see and talk to students. Students however see it as a very real barrier. The same reason is often given for not speaking up in discussion groups, i.e. students are afraid of voicing their opinion lest they should appear foolish. They do not want teachers to know that they have problems because this may draw the teacher's attention to the fact that they are not doing very well.

Although the barrier is a psychological one and is in the mind of the student, teachers by omission often do little to help. Just saying 'if you need any help, let me know' is not really enough. The teacher needs to go out of his way to get to know the students on his course, to be able to talk informally to them and to assess, almost without them knowing, whether they are in need of help and guidance. This leads to the third area which was seen as a problem area in the report, *Learning from Learners* (Parlett *et al*., 1976), namely that intellectual contact was confined to formal teaching.

Intellectual Contact Confined to Formal Teaching

Students and teachers see a need for teachers to be

> tolerant, patient, relaxed, friendly, approachable, they should also be interested in students . . . . be available and willing to help when wanted . . . . Both parties also expressed a wish to get to know each other outside teaching hours . . . . perhaps both parties recognise the present lack of communication between them and are seeking ways of overcoming this. (Hills, 1976)

Although this survey of students' and teachers' expressed perceptions of course needs was taken mainly from American published literature, it does again indicate the changing climate of thought, the need for more informal communication between teachers and students. This problem area is obviously one which has in part contributed to the barrier between teachers and students simply because contact was limit limited to formal teaching only, but it need not be so if the teacher can adopt the more open approach to the student in revealing rather than concealing his own ideas and problems associated with course work. He should attempt to meet and talk to students in a more informal way.

Parlett *et al.* (1976) summarise these feelings as follows:

> Occasions when staff and students are forced into close intellectual collaboration tend to occur naturally in working projects outside the customary lecture and seminar rooms . . . [they] . . . . find themselves, temporarily at least, on the same side of the fence . . . students get to know the staff better, feel more at east, and are more stimulated intellectually; staff tend to acquire more individual appreciation of students and so greater enjoyment for their teaching.

Scrutinising Teaching and Learning

This is the fourth problem area cited in *Learning from Learners*; its basic point is that 'staff and students might engage jointly in an informal investigation of the learning and teaching in which they participate together.' Although the points raised in this section are valid and valuable, it is difficult to see how students, initially at least, possess sufficient information on the methods available to make a substantial contribution. Under this heading I am mainly concerned with how teachers should scrutinise their teaching, in order to provide help to students, leading to a consideration of inputs to the student and outputs from the students as outlined in the previous chapter. Before I discuss this however it will be useful to consider three of the main points raised in *Learning from Learners* (Parlett *et al.*, 1976).

1. 'Underestimating confusion . . .' Teachers frequently over-estimate how much their students comprehend.
2. 'Teaching in too linear a fashion . . . learning often gets out of step with the linear regularity of a lot of teaching.'
3. Overlooking individual differences . . . 'Teaching, for most of the time, is organised on the assumption that students can be thought about in the mass, that they can learn by more or less the same

means.'

These three points essentially summarise what is wrong with traditional teaching methods and what should be taken account of when considering alternative methods, namely:

1. That course work should begin only when the student has sufficient background knowledge, and should continue at a speed sufficient for the student to relate new work to work that he has already understood.
2. That linear teaching as exemplified by the lecture method does not necessarily keep in step with learning, other methods should be considered — this point is taken up again below.
3. That methods should cater for individual differences.

There are now available a variety of teaching and learning methods which attempt in various degrees to take account of these points. Various references can be found giving details of these alternative methods (e.g. Hills, 1976; Goldschmid and Goldschmid, 1973) and details of the recent major books on teaching and learning in higher education are given in the bibliography at the end of this book. Any teacher who is interested in following up these methods more fully and perhaps integrating elements of them into his own courses should consult these references. Rather than explore this more fully here I should like to turn to the inputs to the student listed in Chapter 8 and look at them in terms of the positive help a teacher can give the student to render the communication they provide of maximum value.

Inputs to the Student

1. *From the teacher in charge of the course as information about the timetable, the syllabus, various administrative arrangements etc.* This particular input has been explored elsewhere in this chapter as the need to give the student as much information as possible to help to orientate him to his, at first, new environment and the requirements of the course.

2. *Course content in the form of a series of lectures supplemented by group discussions etc.* The administrative convenience of the lecture has already been mentioned, but what has not been mentioned is that teachers and students appear to like lectures. Teachers seem to like lectures because it gives them a sense of involvement with their students although I believe this to be largely illusory. It may be that teachers like the element of performance in this act of communication with a

large group.

Students sometimes behave as if the lecture is the only real part of the education process and they gain knowledge by some sort of osmosis through sitting through a set of lectures. In fact, the lecture can only display information to the student, it cannot ensure that he learns it. Thus if a teacher has to give a series of lectures the basic requirement as we have seen in previous chapters is that he should put the information across clearly and distinctly. Handout notes giving the main structure of each lecture can help, as can some advice on taking notes from a lecture early on in the course.

Since each teacher has his own style, it is particularly appropriate that he should talk a little to the students on how to take notes from lectures, since only he is likely to know his own style and preferences. One useful way of introducing this topic is to ask students to take outline notes during the first lecture of a series and allow time at the end for the lecturer to hand out his own version of the lecture notes. These can act as a basis for discussion and help to orientate the student's notetaking for the rest of the series.

3. *From the teacher and other students in discussion groups and other forms of group work.* Chapter 6 is particularly concerned with this area, and guidance on the advantages and methods of group work are given there. Teachers should bear in mind particularly that group work is most valuable as a means of encouraging discussion between students, so that they can share their ideas with others.

4. *Directed reading to the student from the teacher.* This is particularly important during the first year of a student's course. It is all too easy to swamp a student by giving him a large reading list and expecting him to apply himself to reading. This is sometimes done without later making any reference to the material or finding out if the student has read it.

The aim of a first-year reading list should be that the student
   (a) realises that the teacher giving the course is for the most part only representing one viewpoint and that there are others
   (b) is directed into a situation where he has to use the library as part of his course
   (c) becomes accustomed to using books and extracting information from them.

A first-year reading list should therefore be carefully prepared so that it is relatively short and directed perhaps to specific sectors or pages in a book (not just the whole book). The material should be integrated with course material and not be an optional extra. A further elementary point, but one that will make the librarian very happy, is to ensure that the material on the reading list is in the library before the course begins.

In later years of a course the purpose of the reading list can change and become much more non-directive as the student gains in confidence and ability.

5. *Information from the teacher to the student on his performance on a piece of practical work, an essay or other assignment that he has completed.* This is concerned with feedback on the outputs from the student and is dealt with under the next heading.

6. *Information received by the student on his performance in short tests or term examinations.* Examinations and tests are normally thought of as tools of assessment, which they are, but they can be used to help the student to consolidate the course work, to inform him of the progress he is making on the course and to provide him with practice in examination technique. If these latter purposes are intended, then it is essential that the teacher should mark the tests or examinations and return them to the student as quickly as possible for maximum benefit.

If tests are to help the student, there is no reason why they should not be self-marked tests. Self-tests of this kind have been described in use with a first-year electrical engineering course as consisting of

firstly a pre-knowledge test, designed to show the student what he should know upon entry to the course, and secondly tests given at predetermined intervals. The latter tests were designed to test material content of the course.

After completing a test, the student was given an answer sheet which enabled him to mark his own answers. Thus he was able to see immediately in which areas his knowledge might be weak. (Hills, 1976)

Examinations used to help the student to acquire good examination technique should be prefaced with reference to old examination papers and to a discussion of examination techniques as outlined in the previous chapter.

7. *Informal inputs from other students.* Inputs of this kind can be helpful when a student experiences the kind of 'psychological barrier'

previously mentioned. It is sometimes difficult for a teacher to appreciate the confusion or lack of comprehension experienced by a student, since the explanation given to the students is obviously quite clear to the teacher. This is where other students who have understood a problem are in a much better position to help than the teacher, because they are mostly working in the same frame of reference as the bewildered student. This point may not necessarily occur to students seeking help, and it does no harm for the teacher to point this out. He might also point out the advantages of an informal group of students working together.

8. *Reading done by the student.* If a student does get as far as admitting to a teacher that he has gaps in his background knowledge, he or she can be given a good introductory text to read. However, it should be borne in mind that what may seem to be a good introductory text to the teacher may not appear so to the student. All too often the gap between the elementary text and the more advanced work of the course appears unbridgeable and it may be wise for the teacher to arrange informal discussions with the student to see how he or she is coping with the work.

The teacher should also remember that the student with problems of background knowledge may not come to him; therefore a general point made to all students on the helpfulness of a good introductory text will not come amiss.

9. *Non-verbal information given largely unconsciously by the teacher.* This has already been dealt with in Chapter 4. It is important that the teacher is at least aware of this channel of communication and makes some attempt to bring it under control, because it is mainly this non-verbal information that tells the student about the teacher's attitude to the work. It also tells him what emphasis the teacher puts on different parts of the course.

The Teacher as Sender

The teacher as sender of the educational message thus has many responsibilities to his students. I particularly like Gilbert Highet's assessment of the general principles of teaching methods given in his book *The Art of Teaching* (1951). His title serves to remind us that, although we have gone some way to making teaching a science, it is still largely up to the individual and his interpretation to render the process effective.

We can point out only a few general principles to make their teaching more effective.

The first is clarity. Whatever you are teaching, make it clear. Make it as firm and as bright as sunlight. Not to yourself — that is easy. Make it clear to the people you are teaching — that is difficult.

The second is patience. Anything worth learning takes time to learn, and time to teach.

The third principle is responsibility. It is a serious thing to interfere with another man's life. It is hard enough to guide one's own.

If the teacher can still bear these principles in mind when surrounded by lecture preparation, a heavy timetable, administrative pressures, not to mention his own research commitments and personal life, then he won't go far wrong!

10 EFFECTIVE TEACHING AND LEARNING

In November 1964, B.F. Skinner gave a lecture to the Royal Society entitled 'The Technology of Teaching' (Skinner, 1968). This was perhaps the forerunner of the term 'educational technology' with its implication that education is now merely a mechanistic process.

Although there is now a whole range of possible interactions, possible not just between teacher and student, but also between a number of other methods and sources of information broadly as summarised below:

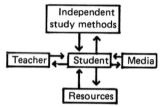

it is, I hope, apparent from this book that we are still far from the point where teaching and learning can be regarded as something apart from human interaction.

Highet (1951) gives us an insight into the qualities of the 'good' teacher and many, if not all, of the qualities that he gives are still true of the 'good' teacher of today. True, the role of the teacher has changed from one of 'dissemination of all knowledge' more towards one of 'manager of resources', but, as we have seen, teachers need to think of themselves in a multiplicity of roles and here qualities of commitment, enthusiasm and understanding are still all-important. Since life is human communication and interaction it is right that this should be so.

The programmed learning movement of the 1960s showed clearly the need for human interaction in the teaching and learning process, as many will remember. In June 1962 I wrote enthusiastically in the *School Science Review*:

> There are many questions as yet unanswered, but whatever the outcome of present researches it is certain that the programmed learning method is an extremely efficient method of teaching. In

industry for imparting practical skills it may become invaluable. In schools and science laboratories it may free the teacher from routine learning processes and enable him to concentrate on those things which a tight examination usually excludes. (Hills, 1962)

At that time I firmly believed that better and more structured programmes gave the answer to the need for more effective learning. I, like many others, was concentrating entirely on passing knowledge embodied in a series of subject courses to the student. The principles of active learning, small units of material, proceeding from the simple to the complex, could be proved to have worked from the results of tests given to students immediately after they had completed the programmed material.

What became apparent very quickly was that programmes, although they were passing information to the student, when taken *en masse*, were producing effects of boredom and strain by overloading the student with what were for the most part long sequences of textual material unrelieved by any other methods.

This is not to deny that the principles of programmed learning worked and still do. These principles are largely those recommended in Chapter 3 represented by the four key words: motivation, activity, understanding and feedback.

In addition to the over-enthusiasm of the 'programmed learners' of the 1960s, the situation was complicated by the over-commercialisation of the process. The number of 'teaching machines' designed to display programmed learning sequences multiplied at a tremendous rate only to come to a rapid and untimely end, because manufacturers were unable or unwilling to ensure a sufficient supply of programmes in a variety of subjects to go with their machines. *The Yearbook of the Association for Programmed Learning and Educational Technology, 1974/5* illustrates this by the following comment: 'Between 1969 and 1971 the number of machines . . . available sank from 30 to 18 . . . the number of new programmes available for teaching machines is quite small'. (Howe and Romiszowski, 1974). In the Year Book for 1976/7 only six actual teaching machines are listed (Howe and Romiszowski, 1976). Because of the unfortunate consequences of the over-commercialisation of the subject, the programmed learning movement was thought to be dead, but in practice it has only changed and adapted. The movement reflected the character of the sixties, a time of change and thought, a time when in a number of fields there was a growing awareness of the student as an individual. It is true that many of the programmed learning sequences of that time were boring and repetitive, but they emphasised the role of the student as learner and made at least some attempt to cater for the needs of the individual student with different levels of understanding and background.

The present educational technology movement embraced principles of programmed learning and brought together facets of systems analysis for planning curriculum development and course structures, audio-visual materials to act as channels of communication, and an awareness of the need to evaluate and modify materials and methods, depending on the reaction of the students. The Council for Educational Technology has defined educational technology as 'not simply the use of new equipment and techniques but also their adoption and coordination to serve new patterns and systems of education' (CET Information Leaflet, 1976). Over the past decade a number of new patterns of learning have developed, and these can be broadly considered under two main headings: those directly involving teacher participation and those self-instructional methods which involve the teacher as manager.

In this book it has perhaps appeared that there has been too heavy an emphasis on the former and not the latter. There have been two main reasons for this. First, self-instructional methods have been described in my book, *The Self-Teaching Process in Higher Education* (Hills, 1976). Second, I feel strongly that, although the new pattern of learning and the methods that are emerging show effective ways of presenting course material and ensuring that students learn, one must never lose sight of the interactive element in the teaching/learning process. This can be regarded as a mere counterweight to the mechanistic aspects of some of the methods that are being developed such as computer-assisted learning or it can be regarded as a more fundamental aspect of the process of education for the transmission of the standards and cultures of our society. However one regards it, it is important. Oettinger (1969), writing on the success of the Postlethwaite Audio Tutorial Method, comments: 'Where comparable talents can be mustered, comparable results may be expected. Where not, the results might well be inferior to those obtained through conscientious teacher-proofing.'

This book has attempted to emphasise the possibilities in the interaction between teacher and student, but it has also attempted to give some guidelines for the preparation of effective teaching/learning material which apply either to teacher-mediated processes or to individualised learning methods.

The following account attempts to distill some of the main points in relation to both the interactions and the guidelines. A full summary of the main points of each chapter has been placed at the end of the book for quick reference to any areas that may particularly interest you. We shall now consider and where necessary regroup the main points under the three headings of our model, teacher processes, channels of communication and student processes.

Teacher Processes

The teacher needs to:

(a) Help students to achieve the transition from school to institutions of higher education both in academic and in personal terms.

(b) Think about course work both in terms of academic content and the needs of the student.

(c) Find out if a student is in a position to be able to receive and understand the material of a course and, if not, to help him.

(d) Determine if a student has the necessary skills to cope with his courses, e.g. notetaking, writing up, skills of discussion and argument and, if not, to help him to acquire them.

(e) Take account of the student's level of growth and physical and intellectual ability.

(f) Arouse the student's interest in the subject material and help him to maintain that interest.

(g) Keep the student aware of his progress.

(h) Be more open about course work and requirements, especially if self-teaching methods are to be used.

(i) Talk informally to students, revealing rather than concealing his own ideas and problems.

(j) Take care not to overestimate the amount that students know.

(k) Be aware of the basic factors in interpersonal and group processes.

(l) Be aware of the non-verbal content of his communications.

Channels of Communication

The main points in this area, although concerned with the channels of communication, can still be considered in terms of teacher actions. The feedback channel is considered under student processes. The teacher needs to:

(a) Display information and ideas in written, spoken or pictorial language.

(b) Be aware of the range of possible media, its availability in his own institution, the availability of suitable content material, and the

appropriateness of its use in his courses.
(c) Be aware of the basic techniques for recording or preparing audio-visual materials.
(d) Make the message as clear and as accurate as possible.
(e) Be aware of verbal and non-verbal processes of communication, both for face-to-face teaching, and when preparing pre-recorded materials.

Student Processes

A useful model of student processes is given by the following:

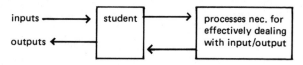

In terms of this model students need to be told or to find out about the types of input and output requirements for a course, for example, conventional teaching or self-instructional methods. They need two main sets of skills to deal with course work, one concerned with the knowledge content, i.e. *students need to have or should acquire sufficient background in subjects that they are studying*, the other concerned with course work and with maintaining their ability to deal with it, i.e. *students need to have or should acquire a variety of skills, e.g. note-taking, writing up, skills of discussion and argument; students need to plan and organise their time; students need to learn how to use a library and to create their own personal data banks.*

The student needs to learn to use the feedback channel of communication. This can be summarised as: *learn to ask if you don't understand, learn to use talk and discussion as a means of learning, learn to be more open to teachers.*

Teacher and Student

We have seen how teaching and learning rather than being a situation of the following type:

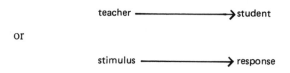

has to take account of the needs and perceptions of the student and should contain a large amount of feedback of information in both directions. Also, apart from the points given under the three headings above, there are three more important general points which teachers and students would do well to hold in their minds when engaging in this communication process. They are:

1. Education is a process by which knowledge, standards, heritage and culture are communicated from generation to generation.
2. Communication is not just talking at others, it is also understanding how they are receiving your message.
3. A period of formal education should not be seen only in terms of short-term aims but also in terms of the need to acquire skills of work and thought that will last for life, i.e. as development towards becoming a self-directed individual.

By chance these three points fit into the three categories of teacher processes, channels of communication and student processes.

The first point serves to remind us that as teachers we are mediators between the accumulated knowledge base, culture and standards of our predecessors and the coming generation.

The second point indicates that mere telling is not enough; the process of communication requires the teacher and the student to be in harmony — good feedback is essential.

The third point is directed toward the student and stresses that he needs to look at his period of formal education in the long term, not just as a series of hurdles that he is being forced to overcome with no benefit for the future.

It is hoped that all these points argue for a closer examination of teaching and learning as a communication process to make it more open and to encourage a closer interaction between teacher and student.

SUMMARY OF THE MAIN POINTS

1 Human Communication and the Education Process

This chapter is concerned to set the scene for the chapters which
follow. The education process is seen as communication between
society and the individual.

Some main educators throughout the centuries from Socrates to
Froebel and Montessori.

These accounts show how echoes of these fundamental concepts occur
in the chapters which follow.

2 Teaching and Learning as a Communication Process

The main purpose of this book is to explore teaching and learning in
terms of a communication process.

In the context of this book communication is defined as the transmission of information between people, animals and machines.

Shannon's communication model was originally applied to the development of electrical systems but can be applied to human
communication.

Teaching and learning are concerned with the teacher as sender of the
message and the student as receiver of the message.

Teacher Provides Input and Coding

Input

Education is a process by which knowledge, standards, heritage and
culture are communicated from generation to generation.

In today's ever-changing world relevance is of great importance.

There is a need to ensure that the content and type of courses are
made the subject of regular review.

Coding

Coding = making input visible to the student.

Ideas and statements must be displayed in writing, pictorially or by the
spoken word. These are reinforced or modified by a variety of non-

verbal messages.

Teachers need to ensure that the student is able to receive, understand and decode material.

Student and teacher should have a common set of symbols that go to make up spoken or written language or pictorial symbols.

There will be no communication unless there is compatability of coding and decoding. Symbols are only representative of events they are not the events themselves.

Channel

This should accurately convey the message to the student.

There are many varieties of auditory and visual equipment now available, ranging from simple aids, e.g. the overhead projector to video-tape players and computer graphics terminals.

The main consideration is that the channel of communication should clearly and accurately convey the message to the student.

Because symbols are only representations of events the channel of communication can never convey the same message as the actual event itself.

The channel also has specific characteristics.

Noise

Many sources of noise in teaching and learning. One source is the teaching environment itself. Factors include: comfort of chairs; colour of walls and floor covering; sound quality and spacial dimensions.

Size of group can contribute physical noise, especially for those sitting at the back.

The teacher is the biggest potential source of noise. To reduce noise as much as possible he must: be clear as to his purpose; ensure that material is clear and unambiguous; choose appropriate channels of communication; use a variety of techniques as appropriate.

Student Decodes Message and Produces Output

A student is expected to have: sufficient background in subjects he is studying, skills of notetaking, writing up and of argument and discussion.

Part of teacher's task is to determine if a student possesses such skills and discuss them with him.

Feedback

An important part of any self-regulating mechanism.

The communication process is dynamic interchange. Student feeds back information on how teacher's message is received. This forms continuous feedback loop, i.e. student keeps teacher aware of difficulties he may be having; teacher keeps student aware of progress and tries to help him solve his difficulties.

Three categories are proposed in the final model: teacher processes (see Chapter 9), channels of communication (see Chapters 3, 4, 5, 6, 7), student processes (see Chapter 8).

3 Psychological Aspects of Communication

Communication either increases a student's knowledge, changes his beliefs, his attitudes or behaviour.

Definition of learning: the process of acquiring knowledge, changing beliefs, attitudes or behaviour.

In the past psychologists have often regarded the teacher/student interaction in terms of stimulus/response only without regard to the human organism involved. Recently interest has centred on the individual and the variety of drives, motives and functions modifying his reception of the message.

Stimulus/Response Theories

Watson

Principle of frequency (more often make a given response to a stimulus more likely to make it again).

Principle of recency (the more recently a response is made the more likely it is to be made again).

Thorndyke

Learning is not simply the strengthening effect of stimulus and response occurring together but depends rather on the effects following the response.

The 'Law of Effect': strengthening occurs when followed by satisfying conditions.

Skinner

He thought principles of frequency and recency were merely 'learning by doing'.

Frequent drill practice should enable a response to be remembered.

He was concerned with 'operant conditioning' which was not behaviour elicited by specific stimuli but behaviour emmited by the organism itself.

His work on the shaping of behaviour has been applied to the teaching and learning process.

He is critical of the infrequency and delay in the reinforcement of material presented to and produced by the students.

His definition of teaching is that the student is 'taught' in the sense that he is induced to engage in new forms of behaviour.

His ideas on linear question and answer sequences became part of the programmed learning movement.

Practical learning principles which emerged from programmed learning are: motivation, activity, reinforcement, limits on the amount of and complexity of material presented.

Gestalt psychologists were concerned not just with the mechanistic aspects of behaviour but the way in which an organism interpreted and perceived stimuli presented to it as a unified whole.

Gestalt (German) = 'form' or 'pattern'

Max Wertheimer

He started the movement and developed the concept of 'insight'.

Insightful learning occurs when one suddenly feels that one really understands.

Kurt Lewin

He was concerned with aspects of motivation, needs and personality.

His 'field theory' of learning is concerned with how a learner gains insight into himself and the things around him and how he then uses these to react to events around him.

Five General Principles for Designing Practical Learning Situations

Learning is effective and permanent (1) when the learner is *motivated*; (2) when the activity is geared to *physical and intellectual ability*; (3) when the learner can see *meaningful relationships* and a goal towards which he is working; (4) when the learner is provided with an indication of how he is progressing (*feedback* on progress); (5) when the learner also experiences satisfactory *personality adjustment and social growth*.

All five are concerned with internal processes of the learner. Most can be directly manipulated by the teacher. Some like maturation are not directly manipulable.

Here we are concerned with the former and consider them under four key words: motivation, activity, understanding and feedback.

Motivation

Concerned with factors of arousal of interest and maintenance of that interest.

Curiosity is a natural trait. Interest aroused if novel stimulus presented, diminished if task becomes repetitive or boring.

Young children — interest aroused and maintained for long periods by the challenge of exploring a new situation.

Adult not so, possibly due to an ability to relate the new situation to existing knowledge thus shortening the time taken to absorb new knowledge.

Need to present material in a way that engages the student in the task and which contains the elements of challenge.

Interest can be maintained by the teacher keeping a feeling of personal contact.

Motivation consists of: presenting the material in an interesting way; personal contact so student is not left to struggle on his own.

Activity

Learning requires some level of activity.

Activity is being built into some of the new individual learning approaches.

What is most important is that the student knows how to be active.

Chapter 8 looks at inputs of information to the student and how he can actively deal with these. It also looks at processes within the student and levels and types of activity that he needs to take.

Understanding

Child is absorbing information from the time he is born.

We all build up a complex set of understandings, i.e. 'frames of reference' — internal models of the world about us.

We try to fit new information into existing frames of reference and there is a tendency to minimise inconsistencies.

Teachers should attempt to ensure that a student receiving new information has sufficient understanding of background and context of communication.

Feedback

There is a need to help the student monitor progress, to give him
continued assurance on his progress.

Essays, tests and examinations are traditionally tools of assessment, i.e.
the teacher sees how the student is getting on. However, it is possible
to use tests to allow the student to monitor his own progress.

Keeping the student informed of progress also keeps teacher and student
in close contact helping to maintain motivation.

Current trends

Bruner, Rogers, Perry, Pask all show concern for the student as an
active processor of information.

Perry gives nine stages of student development: (1) student sees world in
terms of right answers existing for all things; (2-5) student perceives
and accepts diversity of opinion: (6) student sees need to orient himself in relativistic world; (7-9) student makes commitment as an
ongoing unfolding activity through which he expresses his life style.

The way in which student perceives the world will affect the way in
which he processes information.

4 Verbal and Non-verbal Communication

Verbal

Information reaches our ears by sound waves and is then conveyed to
our brains.

The listener gives meaning to the words.

Teacher Talk

It is not just words. One must consider factors of difference in loudness,
tone, pitch, rhythm.

Sound Intensity (decibels)

There is a whole range of sound intensity between quiet whisper (5 dec.)
and pneumatic drill (10 dec.)

Distance

This is a function of loudness. Loudness is a tool that can enhance and
improve verbal communication, i.e. a quiet voice can focus attention at beginning of lecture. Similarly, tone and pitch can be varied.

When we are depressed we tend to talk slower and at a lower pitch, when excited faster and at a higher pitch

The rhythm of the voice can be varied by varying the speed of delivery, by introducing hesitations, repetitions and silences. Rhythm is generally thought of in musical terms but recurrent patterning in speech is generally pleasing, random pattern is generally disturbing.

A boring or soporific voice can lull listeners to sleep. The speed of delivery is important. Normal rate of speaking is 100-200 wds/min. Rather than using a slow distinct rate of delivery, better to speak faster with clarity and introduce hesitations, repetitions or silences.

Voice can reflect inner feelings.

Voice heard by sound conduction through the air. We hear ourselves partly by this, partly by bone conduction — considerable difference.

Student Receives Words

Hearing does not equal listening.

Hearing is sound falling on the ear.

Listening concerns following factors: context, identification, interpretation and relationship to existing knowledge.

Verbal comments can be 'misheard' and if parts of message are missed listener tends to supply missing bits from experience. Clarity of speech and planned repetition of material are important in this context.

It is important that the student has sufficient background information to be able to listen.

The skill in listening is to make oneself interested in material.

Adopting a questioning technique helps.

Listening skills can be improved by any method involving noticing or questioning things said.

Advice to lecturers: say what you are going to say, say it and then say that you have said it, initially directing attention to important things and then confirming their importance.

Teacher/Student Interaction

A good flow of conversation involves — a definite rhythm of length of talk, of speed of reply, a tendency to interrupt etc . . .

When conversation is not going well there is a tendency for the teacher to go on talking so that contact is not broken by awkward silences.

Questioning can draw responses from student and set the conversation in motion. Open-ended questions are better than ones requiring a 'yes/no' answer or choice of alternatives.

The Choice of Words

Words can convey emotional meanings, prejudice, logical fallacies, definitions, facts, habits of thought, suggestion and analogy.

Non-Verbal Communication

Non-verbal signals give emphasis and force to a spoken message, show more accurately what the person speaking really feels.

Emotional state shown by way person holds himself tense or relaxed.

Teacher often is unaware of non-verbal component of the communication. This is dealt with later.

What is Communicated by Non-Verbal Behaviour?

Three main areas:
- (1) to support or deny verbal communication;
- (2) to take the place of verbal communication;
- (3) to show emotions and attitudes.

Head movements are used to illustrate these, e.g. small uncontrolled jerking head movements can show person is in a tense state, e.g. state of rage.

Relaxed people make slow, easy body movements.

Eye contact: important for teachers as this can close personal distance between them and students.

Two people looking into each other's eyes gives a channel of communication. Gives heightened awareness and can express friendship, love, curiosity or hate.

Eye contact can be maintained for long or short time, can be a furtive gaze or open glance.

Long, open gaze = friendship, can become stare and create anxiety by indicating aggression or dislike.

Short glance = dislike or deception.

To avoid threats or being found out people avoid prolonged eye contact.

Speaker may make eye contact when finishes speaking to see how message received by other person.

Eye narrowing = receiver puzzled or afraid.

Size of pupil enlarges if looking at something pleasant.

Many variables and variants, can show non-verbal behaviours: voice variations, head movements, eye variations, hand and foot movements, posture, gait, hesitations and silences, touching, breathing, clothes and dress.

Breathing varies with emotional state and indicates inner feelings.

Breathe faster when afraid, in difficult situations, when tensed up for
    action, heavy when emotionally disturbed.
Dress and state of grooming: unkempt hair, lack of care in dress =
    disturbed inner state; neatly dressed, well groomed = someone in
    control of himself; shows how a person regards himself or how he
    wants to be thought of by others.

The Teacher and Non-Verbal Communication

There is no definitive taxonomy of non-verbal behaviours.
Best advice: each person should investigate his own non-verbal
    behaviour, read up subject and engage in self-observation.
The non-verbal component in teaching should complement and reinforce
    the verbal component.
Continuum of seven categories for non-verbal gestures given from
    'enthusiastic — openly supportive' to 'disapproval'.
Depending on context a non-verbal gesture can change its meaning
    completely, e.g. eye contact can be friendly and supportive or it
    can express disapproval.
Cannot consider non-verbal communication in isolation.
Teachers in groups should 'make contact' with each individual member,
    can do this through eye contact to make students feel that work
    personally involves each of them.
Students may try to avoid such contact by busying themselves sorting
    papers or taking notes — especially if they feel they don't know the
    answer to a question and are afraid they may be called upon to give
    an answer.
Students seek non-verbal cues from teachers as to expectations of
    teachers and relative importance of material presented. This is why
    it is essential teacher sends out helpful messages complementing
    rather than interfering with the verbal component.
Teacher can get information from students: sitting with focused atten-
    tion means student is attending; gazing out of window, or whispering
    — he may have lost the thread of the argument.
Limitations of group method: each student is individual, should
    teacher repeat for some students or continue for majority.
Need to consider the learning environment in communication terms.

5 Audio-Visual Communication

Visual Communication: Teacher's Viewpoint

Teacher concerned to pass information to student clearly and

accurately — does so by coding ideas into symbols — either written
or spoken language or pictorial symbols.

Symbols are representative of events, not the events themselves.

One picture can be worth a thousand words.

Choice of visual media depends on purpose. Choice is from (1) real
objects and 3D models; (2) pictures and drawings; (3) diagrams;
(4) graphs and charts.

(1) Real Objects and Models

Real objects especially in own environment can be valuable.

Difficult to get students out of lecture room and classroom often. Real
objects and events may be too large, small or difficult to bring to
students. 3D models any size more convenient.

(2) Pictures and Drawings

Projected 35mm slide advantage over model can be shown in a variety
of sizes. If different aspects needed several pictures can be prepared.

Drawings advantage over photographs: can be simplified so focusing
attention on specific areas or functions of the real thing.

Drawings are one more step away from the real thing.

(3) Diagrams

A further abstraction from reality: useful in showing how things work
and way in which parts of an object interrelate to make the whole.
Diagrams capable of considerable simplification, and of describing
complex operations by breaking down into simpler units.

(4) Graphs and Charts

Further abstraction — useful to show selected values from tables of
data to show trends clearly.

Pictures, diagrams, charts and graphs can be static or moving.

Visual Communication: Student's Viewpoint

Muller-Lyer illusion showing two apparently different lengths of lines
used to illustrate that what teacher thinks he is communicating may
not be what is received by student. What he receives may not be
what he perceives. This is related to what he is directed to see and
his internal frame of reference.

Two levels of visual communication: (1) conscious appreciation, teacher
directs student to what he should see; (2) unconscious level,
material assimilated by student and subjected to inspection in light
of his previous experience.

Visual Communication: Equipment

Real objects, 3D models, printed page: need no equipment.

Other methods of displaying visual images involve equipment. Main
types of equipment are: (1) still visuals; (2) moving visuals; (3)
combinations; (4) data transmission systems and computers.

Visual Communication — the Preparation of the Material

Real Objects and Models

Student can recognise important parts of real objects by use of models
or abstractions from reality, e.g. diagram or simplified drawing.

Clear educational purpose essential when considering materials to be
used.

Models can retain complex detail, be simplified, be static or movable,
can have removable sections.

Pictures and Drawings

Good photograph can replace inaccessible object, photograph must
give realistic impression.

Avoid distortion.

Remove non-essentials.

Photograph small objects against plain background.

Advantage of drawings — unwanted material can be omitted.

Diagrams, Graphs and Charts

Hand-drawn originals do not make particularly clear slides.

Graphic artist versions clearer, not always necessary, e.g. when a
teacher shows only a hypothesis.

Illustrations from books may be too informative, should be drawn
to show only relevant material.

Written or tabular information should not be too detailed.

Selective values can show a trend: a graph often shows trend even
better.

Audio-Communication

Increasing use being made of pre-prepared material to aid teaching,
in individual self-teaching situations.

Preparation of Material

Voice capable of variations in loudness etc.

In recording use a clear non-monotonous voice.

Use reel-to-reel recorder for master recording, here errors can be
    edited out.

Avoid tape noise — use high tape speed; hum — earth equipment, keep
    microphone from recorder, do not put microphone and recorder on
    same table; distortion — not too high recording volume; inadequate
    treble — clean tape heads; poor acoustic balance — avoid placing
    microphone too far away; excessive sibilants — avoid placing micro-
    phone too close.

The Selection of Audio-visual Media

Selection should be empirical as stated by Hawkridge. No definitive
    guide exists to selection and use of media. Use simplest means con-
    sistent with a particular purpose.

Author's feelings: face-to-face teaching, 'talk and chalk'; support with
    duplicate notes on main points, diagrams, formulae; in group situa-
    tions talk should be supported by duplicated notes.

For self-teaching: directed references to book or use of printed notes.
    Audio-cassette recorder and printed notes reasonably clear way.

Considering audio-visual media, questions are: Is there a need for
    additional audio-visual communication? What is cheapest effective
    solution with regard to what is available in a particular situation?

6 Interpersonal and Group Communication

Process of life consists of communicating with other people singly or
    in groups.

Communicating with others means talking and understanding how
    they receive one's message.

To know others one must know oneself. Others will not feel or react
    in similar ways but reactions may be in similar range.

Maslow gives thirteen characteristics showing range of things to look
    for. Characteristics describe someone aware of and in control of
    himself: a completely self-directed individual open to experience
    and ideas.

People forming groups go through four stages: forming, rebelling,
    norming, co-operating.

Stages in Group Formation

Forming

Members of group unknown to each other probably.

Anxiety in reactions between each other.
Group task may promote inadequacy in those unable to tackle it.
Anxiety can be generated about ground rules.
Number of pressures and uncertainties exist while group is forming.

Rebelling

Members get to know and test each other, some are leaders, others
    followers.
Conflicts arise, a testing and possibly rebellion.

Norming

Members know and accept each other in roles, inner stability forms
    and conflicts resolve.
Group develops acceptable norms of behaviour.

Co-operating

Group develops cohesiveness, co-ordinated energy develops for task.
Continued stability depends on maintenance of other factors:
    group satisfaction; closeness to centre of activities; say in operation
    of group.
On cohesion good communication grows. Role of leader is important.
    Members will support each other.

The Use of the Group as a Teaching/Learning Method

Formal lecture = teacher giving largely uninterrupted discourse.
Communication is largely teacher   student.
In group sessions teacher takes subsidiary role:

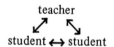

Group work is for discussion between students, saying their feelings,
    thoughts, etc. See how others regard information and their
    interpretation, i.e., they learn to talk freely.
Seven characteristics of small group discussions given: maximum
    interaction; participation by all; think as a group; emergence of
    leadership; broadening of viewpoints, understanding, and
    crystallisation of thought; encourage listening, reflecting, reasoning,
    participating, contributing; allow leadership responsibility to be
    shared.

Varieties of Group Methods

Characteristics above not always apparent, as students unwilling to
 expose themselves and to listen to others. Therefore tutorials often
 turn into mini-lecture.
Many forms of group interaction possible.

Brainstorming

For small groups.

Buzz Groups

For two people or small group.

Case Study Discussions

Discussion of situation or problem, real or fictitious, so that students
 can apply other experiences, develop critical faculties and powers
 of judgement, come to know complex human interactions.

Lecture Discussion

Relationship between teacher and students important for success of this.

Tutorial

Traditional type of group discussion, contrast with seminar. Gap of
 silence often met which can be avoided if students have confidence
 in teacher.

Individual Tutorials

One student/one teacher interaction. Uneconomic. Self-teaching techniques better. Investigations being pursued on interaction between
 student and computer.

Example Classes

Group meets to consider questions. Teacher may consider example
 and group then attempts similar.

Syndicate Groups

Extension of Buzz group.

The Role of the Teacher in Group Work

To ensure the purpose of the group work is fulfilled.
Needs to encourage student to gain confidence.

Should adopt flexible role, mainly as listener.
Should encourage students to produce own ideas, avoiding correcting unless necessary, and not dominating discussion.
Three basic teacher styles: authoritarian; democratic; non-directive.
When adopting directive role, he should start a discussion, maintain it, close it.

7 Varieties of Mass Communication

Everyday information, attitudes etc. influenced by mass communication: newspapers, radio etc.
Face-to-face communication is a two-way exchange of information.
Mass communication is a one-way flow of information. This is concerned with entertainment and flow of knowledge. Mass communication can shape attitudes.
Messages from mass communication system appear in regular units of material.
Regular exposure to, e.g. newspaper, may have cumulative effect. Watson's principle of frequency applies.
Mass-communication systems act in stimulus/response way. Akin to lecture disregarding individual differences. Individuals with different needs etc. make up audience.

Newspapers

Gutenberg inventor of movable type printing press.
Fast modern presses and developments such as computer set type, links via satellite spread news quickly.
Newspapers today mixture of news, advertising, features etc. Magazines tend to be more specialist.
Latter now popular, carry news articles, setting topics against world events or reports, and educational topics.
Most people read newspapers, emphasis on news; magazines are read for entertainment and specialist information.

Radio

1922 British Broadcasting Company.
1927 British Broadcasting Corporation.
Coming of television caused change of radio image.

Television
1930 first BBC Television, in abeyance during Second World War, re-opened, and in 1954 joined by commercial television.
1962 second BBC channel, 1967 colour transmission.
Emphasis on entertainment, but educational content not lacking, e.g. Open University, schools broadcasts.

Film
Television and film same basic function.
Film in pure form like a book concerned with painting a picture of an event on a broad canvas.

Books
Books = first means of educational mass communication.
Most courses use some form of printed materials.
Books need no further equipment. They give a record of events, can be skimmed through quickly, used for random access; convenient for individual study.
Paperback revolution in 1935, low pricing, educational possibility considerable. Important for student to build up own store of books.

Advertising
All-pervasive. Message is persuasion.
Four basic conditions: key words: exposure, perception, retention, decision.
Advertising conditions seen like those of the teaching/learning process.

Implications for Teaching and Learning
Educational value of mass communication systems secondary, main aim for entertainment and selling.
All mass communication is a one-way flow, good teaching and learning give opportunity for feedback.
To get over problem of immediacy of mass communication, recording on audio- or video-cassette recorders for later use possible.
Television transmits less information than is possible to access from a book in the same time.
Television can extend range of communication by providing colour pictures and by communicating non-visual information.

Future Trends
PRESTEL. Possibilities of local centres, many educational possibilities

as unlike CEEFAX and ORACLE, PRESTEL can be interrogated.
Possible future development of an 'information utility', a possible
  communication system accessing information from a large store of
  material as receiver wants it.

8   The Student as Receiver

Long-term aim of educational system is development of student as
    self-directed individual.
Student sees courses in immediate terms.
Student as receiver seen as input/output model.

Inputs

(1) From teacher.
(2) Course content — lectures.
(3) From teacher and students in group work.
(4) Directed reading.
(5) Information on performance in assignments.
(6) Information on performance in tests and examinations.
(7) Informal inputs from other students.
(8) Background reading.

Outputs

(1) Questions and replies by student.
(2) Short presentations by students.
(3) Written assignments, practical work etc.
(4) Completion of test or examination.

Processes Necessary for Dealing Effectively with Input/Output

Inputs considered in Chapter 9 and elsewhere.
Outputs considered as verbal and audio-visual communication in
    Chapters 4 and 5 respectively.
'How to study' books useful for 'hints and tips'.
Effective study ultimately considered by student in his own terms,
    but he should:
(1) Recognise and make best use of teaching methods encountered.
(2) Recognise the value of learning strategies.
(3) Predict, plan and organise the use of his time.
(4) Know how to listen and take notes from lectures.
(5) Create and use a personal 'data bank'.

(6) Know how to use libraries efficiently.

(7) Know how to read books and take notes from them.

(8) Know how to prepare for examinations.

(9) Recognise and be able to use good spoken and written styles of communication.

(10) Adopt appropriate physical conditions for study.

(11) Understand aspects of attention, perception, memory and personal work rhythms.

9 The Teacher as Sender

Lecture convenient for speed, administration, manpower, but educational process should be for benefit of student not convenience of teacher.

Student should be helped to become a 'self-directing individual' and needs: a body of positive knowledge; to be trained to collect evidence; form a balanced judgement; fortify ability to think for himself (Mountford).

Teacher there to ensure communication passed clearly with minimum 'noise'.

Teacher cast in role of 'manager' and 'father figure'.

Teacher's wider role as a student of motivation, a promoter of learning, an observer of growth, craftsman and technician, administrator and therapist (Fleming).

Five main problem areas: the transition from school to university; inadequate exchange of information with students; the 'psychological barrier'; intellectual contact confined to formal teaching; scrutinising teaching and learning. Many teaching and learning methods now coming into use take account of these factors.

Inputs to Student

They have been given in Chapter 8 summary.

The Teacher as Sender

Teacher has many responsibilities to his students.

Highet gives three principles to guide teachers: whatever you are teaching, make it clear; anything worthwhile takes time to learn and time to teach; it is serious thing to interfere with another man's life — it is hard enough to guide one's own.

10   Effective Teaching and Learning

Main points from previous chapters in terms of interactions between
  teacher and student, in terms of guidelines for preparation of
  effective teaching/learning materials.
Points are considered under three headings: teacher processes; channels
  of communication; student processes.

BIBLIOGRAPHY

Abercrombie, M.L. Johnson, 1969, *The Anatomy of Judgement,*
  Penguin Books, Harmondsworth.
Argyle, M., 1967, *The Psychologic of Interpersonal Behaviour,*
  Penguin Books, Harmondsworth.
Beal, G.M., Bohlen, J.M. and Raudabaugh, J.N., 1962, *Leadership and Dynamic Group Action,* Iowa State University Press, Ames, Iowa.
Birdwhistell, R., 1952, *Introduction to Kinesics,* University of
  Louisville Press.
Bligh, D., Ebrahim, G.J., Jaques, D. and Warren Piper, D., 1975,
  Teaching Students, Exeter University Teaching Services, Exeter.
Bockus, H.W., 1969, *Advertising Graphics: A Workbook and Reference for the Advertising Artist,* Collier-Macmillan, London.
Broadley, M., 1970, 'The Conduct of Seminars', *Universities Quarterly,*
  Summer 1970, pp. 274-5.
Bugelski, B.R., 1956, *The Psychology of Learning,* Holt Rinehart and
  Winston, New York.
Buzan, T., 1974, *Use Your Head,* British Broadcasting Corporation,
  London.
Carmichael, L., Hogan, H.P. and Waters, A., 1932, 'An Experimental
  Study of the Effect of Language on the Reproduction of Visually
  Perceived Form', *Journal of Experimental Psychology,* 15, p. 73.
Carnegie Commission, 1973, *Final Report,* Carnegie Commission for
  Higher Education, USA.
Cox, D.F., 1964, 'Clues for Advertising Strategists' in Dexter, L.A.
  and White, D.M. (eds), *People, Society and Mass Communication,*
  Collier-Macmillan, London, pp. 359-94.
Davitz, J.R., 1964, *The Communication of Emotional Meaning,*
  McGraw-Hill, New York.
Dunning, G.G., 1971, 'Research in Non-Verbal Communication',
  Theory into Practice, 10, 4, October 1971, pp. 250-8
Entwistle, N. and Hounsell, D., 1975, *How Students Learn: Implications for Teaching in Higher Education,* Institute for Research into
  Post-Compulsory Education, University of Lancaster.
Erickson, C.W.H., 1965, *Fundamentals of Teaching with Audio-Visual
  Technology,* Macmillan, New York.
Exline, R., 1963, 'Explorations in the Process of Person Perception',

Journal of Personality, 31, pp. 1-20.

Fast, J., 1971, *Body Language*, Pan Books, London.

Fleming, C.M., 1968, *Teaching: A Psychological Analysis*, Methuen, London.

Golby, M., Greenwald, J. and West, R., 1975, *Curriculum Design*, Croom Helm, London.

Goldschmid, B. and Goldschmid, M., 1973, 'Individual Instruction in Higher Education: A Review', *Higher Education*, 3, pp. 1-24.

Hall, E.T., 1959, *The Silent Language*, Doubleday, New York.

Harris, A., Lawn, M. and Prescott, W., 1975, *Curriculum Innovation*, Croom Helm, London.

Hawkridge, D.G., 1973, 'Media Taxonomies and Media Selection' in Budgett, R. and Leedham, J. (eds), *Aspects of Educational Technology VII*, Pitman Publishing, London, pp. 166-77.

Haynes, L., Groves, P., Moyes, R. and Hills, P., 1977, *Effective Learning: A Practical Guide for Students*, Tetradon Publications, Bridge House, Shalford, Guildford.

Highet, G., 1951, *The Art of Teaching*, Methuen, London.

Hills, P.J., 1962, 'Teaching Machines and Science', *School Science Review*, 63, 151, pp. 604-13.

Hills, P.J., 1966, 'A Comparison of Spoken and Linear-Paper-Programme Based Lessons', unpublished MSc thesis, University of Sheffield.

Hills, P.J., 1973, *Study to Succeed*, Pan Books, London.

Hills, P.J., 1976, *The Self-Teaching Process in Higher Education*, Croom Helm, London.

Hodge, R.L., 1971, 'Interpersonal Classroom Communication Through Eye Contact', *Theory into Practice*, 10, 4, October 1971, pp. 264-7.

Hooper, R., 1975, *Two Years On: The National Development Programme in Computer-Assisted Learning*, Council for Educational Technology, London.

Hooper, R. and Toye, I., 1975, *Computer Assisted Learning in the U.K.:*

Howe, A. and Romiszowski, A.J., 1974, *APLET Yearbook of Educational and Instructional Technology*, 1974/75, Kogan Page, London.

Howe, A. and Romiszowski, A.J., 1976, *APLET International Yearbook of Educational and Instructional Technology*, 1976/77, Kogan Page, London.

Some Case Studies, Council and Education Press, London.

Kemp, J.E., 1971, 'Which Medium?', *Audio-Visual Instruction*, December 1971, pp. 32-6.

Kornhauser, A., 1975, 'Computer Assisted Instruction in Chemical

Education' in Rao, C.N.R. (ed.), *Educational Technology in the Teaching of Chemistry*, International Union of Pure and Applied Chemistry, Oxford.

Leith, G.O.M., 1969, *Second Thoughts on Programmed Learning*, National Council for Educational Technology, London.

Love, A.M. and Roderick, J.A., 1971, 'Teacher Nonverbal Communication: The Development and Field Testing of an Awareness Unit', *Theory into Practice*, 10, 4, October 1971, pp. 295-9.

Maslow, A.H., 1962, *Towards a Psychology of Being*, Van Nostrand, Princeton.

Miller, G.A., 1956, 'The Magical Number Seven, Plus or Minus Two: Some Limits on our Capacity for Processing Information', *Psychological Review*, 63, pp. 81-7.

Mountford, J., 1966, *British Universities*, Oxford University Press.

Oettinger, A.G., 1969, *Run Computer Run: The Mythology of Educational Innovation*, Harvard University Press, Cambridge, Mass.

Parker, E.B., 1973, 'Technological Change and the Mass Media' in Pool, I., Frey, F.W., Schramm, W., Macoby, N. and Parker, E.B. (eds), *Handbook of Communication*, Rand McNally, Chicago.

Parlett, M., Simons, H., Simmonds, R. and Hewton, E., 1976, *Learning from Learners: A Study of the Student's Experiences of Academic Life*, The Nuffield Foundation, London.

Peddiwell, J.A., 1939, *The Saber-tooth Curriculum*, McGraw-Hill, New York.

Perry, W.G., 1970, *Ethical Development in the College Years: A Scheme*, Holt Rinehart and Winston, New York.

Potter, F. and Hills, P.J., 1976, 'Self-Directed Learning for 16 to 19 Year-olds', *Trends in Education*, 2, pp. 17-21.

Powell, L.S., 1970, *A Guide to the Use of Visual Aids*, British Association for Commercial and Industrial Education, London.

Power, T.V., 1971, 'Folklore of Teaching Aids', *Vocational Aspects of Education*, 23, 56, pp. 109-13.

Rumelhart, D.E., 1977, *Introduction to Human Information Processing*, John Wiley, New York.

Scheflen, A., 1964, 'The Significance of Posture in Communication Systems', *Psychiatry*, 27, pp. 316-31.

Skinner, B.F., 1968, *The Technology of Teaching*, Appleton-Century-Crofts, New York.

Tansey, P.J. and Unwin, D., 1969, *Simulation and Gaming in Education*, Methuen, London.

Thorpe, L.P. and Schmuller, A.M., 1954, *Contemporary Theories of*

Learning, Ronald, New York.

Thouless, R.H. 1953, *Straight and Crooked Thinking*, Pan Books, London.

Tolansky, S., 1964, *Optical Illusions*, Pergamon Press, Oxford.

Vale, E., 1973, *The Technique of Screenplay Writing*, Souvenir Press, London.

Victoria, J., 1971, 'A Language for Affective Education', *Theory into Practice*, 10, 4, October 1971, pp. 300-4.

Williams, R., 1976, *Communications*, 3rd edn, Penguin Books, Harmondsworth.

FURTHER READING

The following references are mainly in addition to those cited in the text and have been selected not because they represent all that has been written on each subject but are to enable you to pursue the subjects of previous chapters in more depth.

Psychological Aspects of Communication

Broadbent, D.E., 1958, *Perception and Communication*, Pergamon Press, Oxford.

Lindren, H.C., 1969, *The Psychology of College Success: A dynamic approach*, John Wiley, London.

Miller, G.A., 1969, *The Psychology of Communication: Seven Essays*, Penguin Books, Harmondsworth.

Parry, J., 1967, *The Psychology of Human Communication*, University of London Press.

Powell, L.S., 1969, *Communication and Learning*, Elsevier, London.

Verbal Communication

Argyle, M., Alkema, F. and Gilmoor, R., 1971, 'The Communication of Friendly and Hostile Attitudes by Verbal and Non-verbal Signals, *European Journal of Psychology*, 1, 3, pp. 385-402.

Clevenger, T. and Matthews, J., 1971, *The Speech Communication Process*, Scott Foreman & Co., Illinois.

Gartner, J.E., 1972, 'A Study of Verbal, Vocal and Visual Communication', *Dissertation Abstracts International*, 33 (5-B), November 1972, pp. 2343-4.

Ross, R.S., 1974, *Speech Communication: Fundamentals and Practice*, 3rd edn, Prentice Hall, Englewood Cliffs, New Jersey.

Non-Verbal Communication

Galloway, C.M., 1971, 'The Challenge of Non-verbal Research', *Theory into Practice*, 10, 4, October 1971, pp. 310-14.

Hall, E.T., 1966, *The Hidden Dimension*, Doubleday, New York.

Knapp, M.L., 1971, 'The Role of Non-verbal Communication in the Classroom', *Theory into Practice*, 10, 4, October 1971, pp. 243-9.

Koch, R., 1971, 'The Teacher and Non-verbal Communication', *Theory into Practice*, 10, 4, October 1971, pp. 231-42.

Audio-Visual Communication

Dale, E., 1969, *Audio-Visual Methods in Teaching*, 3rd edn, Holt Rinehart and Winston, New York.

Read, H., 1972, *Communication: Methods for all Media*, University of Illinois Press.

Thompson, J.J., 1969, *Instructional Communication*, American Book Co., New York.

Wiman, R.V. and Meierhenry, W.C. (eds), 1969, *Educational Media: Theory into Practice*, Charles E. Merrill, Columbus, Ohio.

Woelfle, R.M., 1975, *A Guide for Better Technical Presentations*, IEEE Press, New York.

Interpersonal and Group Communication

Beckenbach, E.F. and Tompkins, C.B. (eds), 1971, *Concepts of Communication: Interpersonal, Intrapersonal and Mathematical*, John Wiley, New York.

Berne, E., 1964, *Games People Play: The Psychology of Human Relationships*, Grove Press, New York.

Filley, A.C., 1975, *Interpersonal Conflict Resolution*, Scott Foreman & Co., Illinois.

Goldberg, A.A. and Larson, C.E., 1975, *Group Communication*, Prentice Hall, Englewood Cliffs, New Jersey.

Matson, F. and Montagu, A. (eds), 1967, *Human Dialogue: Perspectives on Communication*, Free Press, New York.

The Student as Receiver

Haynes, L., Groves, P., Moyes, R. and Hills, P.J., 1977, *Effective Learning: A Practical Guide for Students*, Tetradon Publications, Bridge House, Shalford, Guildford.

Lingren, H.C., 1969, *The Psychology of College Success*, John Wiley, London.

Parker, L.R. and French, R.L., 1971, 'A description of student behaviour: Verbal and Non-verbal, *Theory into Practice*, 10, 4, October 1971, pp. 276-81.

Pauk, W., 1974, *How to Study in College*, 2nd edn, Houghton Mifflin, Boston.

The Teacher as Sender

Abbey, D.S., 1973, *Now See Hear! Applying Communications to Teaching, Profiles in Practical Education No. 9*, The Ontario Institute for Studies in Education, Toronto.

Cummings, S.N., 1971, *Communication for Education*, Intertext,
  Toronto.

Effective Teaching and Learning

Beard, R., 1972, *Teaching and Learning in Higher Education*, 2nd edn,
  Penguin Books, Harmondsworth.
Bligh, D.A., 1972, *What's the Use of Lectures?* Penguin Books,
  Harmondsworth.
Bligh, D.A. *et al.*, 1975, *Teaching Students*, University of Exeter
  Teaching Services, University of Exeter, Devon.
Davies, I.K., 1971, *The Management of Learning*, McGraw Hill, London.
Entwistle, N. and Hounsell, D. (eds), 1975, *How Students Learn*,
  Institute for Research and Development in Post-Compulsory Educa-
  tion, University of Lancaster.
Heim, A., 1975, *Teaching and Learning in High Education*, NFER, The
  Mere, Slough.
Hills, P.J., 1976, *The Self-Teaching Process in Higher Education*, Croom
  Helm, London.
MacKenzie, N., Postgate, R. and Scupham, J., 1976, *Open Learning:
  Systems and Problems in Post-Secondary Education*, UNESCO,
  Paris.
MacKenzie, N., Eraut, M. and Jones, H.C., 1976, *Teaching and Learning:
  An Introduction to New Methods and Resources in Higher Education*,
  2nd edn, UNESCO, Paris.

Generally Useful References on Communication

Berlo, D.K., 1960, *The Process of Communication: An Introduction to
  Theory and Practice*, Holt Rinehart and Winston, New York.
Cherry, C., 1966, *On Human Communication: A Review, a Survey and
  a Criticism*, 2nd edn, MIT Press, Cambridge, Mass.
Emmert, P. and Brooks, W.D. (eds), 1970, *Methods of Research in
  Communication*, Houghton Mifflin, New York.
Fabun, D., 1968, *Communication: The Transfer of Meaning*, revised
  edn, Glencoe Press, Toronto.
Pool, I., Frey, F.W., Schramm, W., Macoby, N. and Parker, E.B. (eds),
  Handbook of Communication, Rand McNally, Chicago.

INDEX